DEAR MISS VICKIE,

I TRIED YOUR CHIPS FOR THE FIRST TIME. JUST THE ONE TASTE HAS ME CONVERTED FOR LIFE. THESE ARE THE BEST CHIPS ON THE MARKET. WITHOUT THE SALT AND HEAVY OIL, THEY MAKE THE PERFECT SNACK

I WISH YOU THE BEST O...
LUCK IN YOUR
THANK
GREAT

POTATOE CHIPS
market today
friend I was vis...
I was hooked,
first bite, I ha...
se. Whenever I ...
with me, and a ...
say every perso...

in Homemakers
y, etc. One thin...
your fortitude to
price of the...

/Sir

While visiting some frie...

us they served Miss Vick...
...d Cooked chips and to ...
...true what a difference ...
...s to taste such a chip ...
... so just a line

potato chip! ... on a great
market for years to come.

Best of the year
and many more
to come.

January 02 1990.
Dear Miss Vickie,

I really enjoy your wonderful hand-made potato chip. I find them to be a lot better than Hostess, Ruffles or the No-Name Brand.
I'm sure everyone appreciates you (and your farm) bringing an excellent potato chip to the market to make the television selections a lot more interesting.
Take Care, and continued success to you ...
wonde...

...was given som...
...le by a fri...
...lutely delici...
...egful.
...un a bar -
...chased sever
...ouigo Store -
...served som
²PPY have
...nanimous in
...our chips we
I have since

Aug. 21/90

Dear MISS V

Today I bought a bag of Your Chips.
I really liked them.
My mom read Your Story to me. I wanted to write to You, So I did.
...ease write back.
Love Jennifer Wilson,
Age 7,

Dear Miss Vickie:
This is the first time in my life that I've written to any company that produces food products
Of all the current brands of chips that I have tr...
to date, yours is the best made so far.
As in any new product on the market, I was stil...
very skeptical about "hand made potatoe chips". I'm
tried another brand made locally in St. Jacobs, bu...
they were too salty.
Your chips come as close to "french fries" flav...
as humanely possible and your use of sea salt ...
perfect (not enough nor too much).
Now, since hand made chips do cost a bit mo...
...'t mind paying the extra, here co...
...french fries,

DEAR MISS VICKIE

THANK YOU VERY MUCH FOR THE BEST CHIPS EVER. THEY ARE GREAT!

I AM AN OLD CHIP LOVER BUT NOW I AM SPOILED THAT I DON'T LIKE THE TASTE OF ANY OTHER KIND ANY LONGER.

THE ONLY PRESENT PROBLEM IS THAT THEY ARE SOMETIMES HARD TO FIND SO WH... ...CATE A STORE THAT SELLS THEM I... ...UP. ...E — DO

Dear Miss Vickie's *Hand Made Chips*   July 14/89

Your chips are so delicious! My Best frie...

I got a big bag and same night we ate them...

I think your chips are...

...lest in the ~~tuisine~~ b...

They are so crunchy a...

good I feel like eating...

eating more.

Whenever I ~~what~~ wan...

chips I have Miss V...

Chips! will never st...

(buying them!)

here is my ...ess you... want case to write back!

Miss Vickie's
R R #2
New Lowell, Ontario

Dear Miss Vickie,
    I have tried differen... of potato chips before and yours... the No. 1. Aside from rich... vitamin C and cholesterol free ta... and crunchiness is superb compare... other chips that I have tasted. i... from now on I'll stick to your c...

March 26/90

Dear Miss Vickie
    or Whom it May Concern

~~It~~ was given some of your chips to sample by a friend. I found them absolutely delicious, fresh, tasty, just wonderful.
    I run a bar - restaurant in Montreal. purchased several bags from my loc... Provigo Store - (so happy to find them. I served some to my customers fo... happy hour, the customers, as I were unanimous in saying how wonderful your chips were.
    I have since bought them several ti... and given them to friends. Everyone... thinks they are just wonderful.
    You certainly have lots of... here in Montreal, myself... now a regular buy...
    keep u...

MARCH 26/90

Miss and Mr. Vickie's
R. R. # 2
New Lowell, Ontario
L0M 1N0

Dear Miss Vickie:
    I wanted to write and tell you how delicious y... chips are. I am a true chip lover and recently disco... at a store called Scatallons Deli in Grimsby, Ontario. We... ...and the lack of additives and preservatives. ...sure. Thank you for your efforts.
                                                        Sincerely,

Miss Vickie's
KITCHEN

FAMILY RECIPES FROM VICKIE KERR,
CREATOR OF
Miss Vickie's Potato Chips

Vickie Kerr

MISS VICKIE'S KITCHEN

Figure 1

Vancouver / Berkeley

Cataloguing data available from Library and Archives Canada
ISBN 978-1-927958-15-5 (hbk.)

Editing by AnnMarie MacKinnon
Copy editing and index by Lana Okerlund
Cover and interior design by Naomi MacDougall
Front cover photograph by Michael McNamara
Food photographs (interior and back cover) by John Sherlock
except pages 32, 53, 59, 103, and 107 © Thinkstock
Background photographs on pages 1, 11, 39, 55, 75, and 115 © Thinkstock
Photographs on pages viii, xi, and xiv–xv provided by the author
Printed and bound in Canada by Friesens
Distributed in the U.S. by Publishers Group West

Figure 1 Publishing Inc.
Vancouver BC Canada
www.figure1pub.com

FOR
Mary Kerr

My inspiration for this recipe book came from my husband Bill's mother, Mary Kerr, of Alliston, Ontario. At ninety-seven years old, Mary continues to live in her own home. Over the years, she has always been willing to teach me whatever I wanted to learn about preparing food, and especially baking. I love to bake today because of her example and the taste of the wonderful desserts she created. My initial motivation to learn to bake was to delight and please her son. Today I bake for sheer pleasure and joy. Thank you, Mary, with all my heart!

TO MY
Potato Chip Lovers

This book is also dedicated to potato chip lovers everywhere, especially Miss Vickie's Chips customers from 1987 to 1993. On the back of my chip package, I invited customers to write to me to let me know how they enjoyed my handmade potato chips.

Their "Letters to Miss Vickie" encouraged me to continue to offer the highest-quality potato chip with them in mind. Many wrote that they had stopped eating potato chips because of the preservatives, additives, and hydrogenated oil that chip manufacturers used in the 1980s, but after tasting Miss Vickie's and reading the simple ingredients, they had become potato chip lovers again!

The letters came pouring in from the first week in business, and late each night, after making chips all day or driving to sales calls, I would sit down at my desk to read them. I was always inspired by the time these customers took and the thoughtfulness they displayed to put their appreciation down on paper and find a stamp to send it to me in the mail (this was before e-mail!). It was a deep pleasure to answer them all personally.

I cherished the letters so much that I have kept them now for over twenty-five years, and some are included in this book. They are important reminders to me that my customers made my business a success, and they are a validation of the Miss Vickie's Chips story no matter how many years pass.

THIS BOOK IS DEDICATED TO
Bill Kerr
(1949–1997)

On my birthday the year after we retired from operating Miss Vickie's Ltd., my husband, Bill, presented me with a special gift: a gold pen in a velvet-lined box. He had had my name engraved on it, and he gently handed it to me with the express wish that I use it to write a book. Bill told me he hoped I would share the Miss Vickie's story and my experiences during those challenging and rewarding years of starting and building the company to encourage others to follow their dream. The love and friendship we shared during both lean years and times of abundance shaped the woman I am today. He was my mentor and my cheerleader, and he encouraged me during difficult times by quietly reminding me, "Vickie, if it was easy to do, everyone would be doing it."

There have been times while I worked on this book that felt like I was sharing a love story, because he was always part of everything I did. He was cherished by family and friends for his generous and accepting spirit. He was a dedicated partner in family and business, and his resilient nature and positive approach to life influenced me to believe that following my dream was what my life could be about. He always had my back, and I miss him.

Bill and I were blessed with four loving children who are close to my heart and still gather with me around the dinner table on a Sunday. This book is also dedicated to them.

Twenty-five years ago, the recipe for my Miss Vickie's Chips came about because I wanted to create a new and healthier snack for our four young children using the potatoes their father grew. Now our children have inspired me to create something new again. This collection of recipes is designed for them and my future grandchildren.

Miss Vickie's Kitchen contains treasured family recipes and some of the Miss Vickie's Chips history in photos and letters. Completing this book was possible only with the support and encouragement of a few close friends and my family. In particular, our four grown children, Rab, Liam, Dylan, and Angela, provided support and encouragement to me on so many levels. Our children helped out, too, by eating all the dishes I prepared and photographed while the book was taking shape.

And, just like their father did on the farm, the kids know exactly where they can always find me: in the kitchen!

The potatoes getting brushed and washed

Vickie on the farm

Here she is-Miss Vickie (Kerr)

From farm wife to entrepreneur

Potato chip production

Sliced potatoes falling into the kettle

Taste-testing event with our sampling display

Vickie and Bill checking the yield in the potato field

Vickie in front of the family barn

A LETTER FROM
Miss Vickie

WHILE I collected my family recipes for this book, I recalled with nostalgia the days I spent on the farm. Three decades ago, when I was a young farmwife, we were sustained by what was prepared in our own homes and in the homes of family members. Those were less hurried times, when the family gathered to share homemade meals before going out into the world or after returning home from a day at work or school. A thermos of piping hot cocoa, tea, or coffee or a brown-bag lunch made at home and carried with us throughout our day was a simple reminder of our home kitchen. Because dining out is so commonplace these days, many of us accept or don't give much thought to the idea that complete strangers prepare the food we eat.

Preparing and cooking food at home can be simple. It offers us an opportunity to express who we are and where we're from in a unique way. Home cooking can help us discover the many facets of our personal history and creativity. I discovered that preparing food with love for my family and friends became a spiritual experience, too. Recipes and their secrets are handed down by word of mouth from our grandparents, from our parents, and then to us if we listen. Sometimes they are written down, but often they are never recorded. Many of us rely on family recipes and preparation techniques daily without recognizing the valuable legacy of knowledge passed from one man or woman to another. Our personal memories of sharing food around the table are often attached to the flavour of a favourite dish.

This book includes traditional recipes I picked up while growing up in Quebec as well as recipes from the Ontario farm culture where I learned to become a farmwife. I've set out to offer simple recipes that are easy to follow for those who have never baked or cooked before but are willing to try. I have also included several recipes I created over the years to respond to the changing tastes of my four children. And, while we all know it's important to eat healthy foods, this book is not filled with health food recipes. Although I often don't cook with salt, I have included sea salt in some recipes—it should always be considered optional. My conviction is that food should be sourced locally and organically and prepared in season.

In this book, I have collected, recorded, and preserved our family's legacy through the food prepared in our family kitchen. If readers take anything away from this book, I hope it's the knowledge that when we prepare food with and for those we love, using our own two hands, we take part in extending a legacy. And when we eat from someone else's table, let's kiss the precious hands of that cook and give thanks to him or her!

— Vickie Kerr

Grandma's apron

Grandma icing a pan of her brownie recipe

Fresh chips were delivered every day from the farm to the store

Kerr family farmhouse, from 1900 to 1975

Potato field in bloom

Miss Vickie's mascot handing out bags of chips at a parade

Contents

APPETIZERS

Tomato Basil Bruschetta 2

Artichoke Spinach Dip 5

Salsa 6

Guacamole 7

Devilled Eggs 8

SALADS AND SIDES

Easy Spinach Salad 12

Iceberg Lettuce Salad 13

Kale and Spinach Salad 15

Cabbage Salad 16

Egg Salad 17

Cauliflower Salad 18

Vickie's Tuna Salad 21

Wild Salmon Salad 22

Potato Salad 23

Boiled New Potatoes with Butter 24

Bill's Pan-Fried Potatoes 26

Creamy Garlic Whipped Potatoes 28

Vickie's Potato Chips 31

Oven-Roasted Herb Potatoes 33

Twice-Baked Potatoes 35

Quinoa Pilaf 36

SOUPS, STEWS, AND CASSEROLES

Chicken Stock 40

Vegetable Soup 41

French Onion Soup 42

French Canadian Pea Soup 45

Irish Canadian Beef Stew 46

Kowalski Cabbage Rolls 49

Shepherd's Pie 50

Macaroni and Beef Casserole 52

MEAT AND SEAFOOD

Meatloaf 56

Spaghetti Sauce 57

Corned Beef and Cabbage 58

Prime Rib au Jus 60

Montreal Dry Garlic Spareribs 62

Chicken Kiev 65

Roast Chicken and Gravy 66

Apple-Stuffed Pork Loin Roast 68

Baked Wild Salmon 69

Fish and Chips 71

Shrimp Tacos 73

DESSERTS AND BAKING

Chocolate-Covered Potato Chips 76

Potato Chip Chocolate Squares 78

Apple Crisp 79

Nanaimo Bars 81

Chocolate Chip and Nut Cookies 82

Granddad's Cookies 84

Shortbread Cookies 85

Oatmeal Raisin Cookies 86

Grandma Kerr's Brownies 87

Carrot Cake 89

Flourless Chocolate Cake 90

One-Bowl Birthday Cake 92

Tea Biscuits 93

Cranberry Orange Scones 94

Vickie's Baked Granola 97

Zucchini Loaf 98

Banana Muffins 101

Bran Muffins 102

Best Pie Crust 104

Apple Pie 106

Lemon Meringue Pie 108

Pumpkin Pie 109

Lemon Curd Tarts 111

Raspberry Tarts 112

PRESERVING AND PICKLING

Freezer Jam 116

Berries in Syrup 117

Rhubarb Sauce 118

Freezer Sweet Corn Kernels 119

Pickled Beets 120

Garlic Dill Pickles 121

Metric Conversion Charts 122

Index 125

Tomato Basil Bruschetta 2
Artichoke Spinach Dip 5
Salsa 6
Guacamole 7
Devilled Eggs 8

Appetizers

Tomato Basil Bruschetta

YIELD: 16 SLICES, SERVES 4-6 AS AN APPETIZER

A simple-to-make appetizer that's also perfect as a midnight snack for two night owls.

. . . .

4 plum tomatoes or 12 cherry tomatoes, chopped

2 cloves garlic, finely chopped

3 Tbsp chopped fresh basil

3 Tbsp finely chopped red onion (optional)

¼ cup chopped black olives (optional)

1 tsp fresh lemon juice

2 Tbsp extra virgin olive oil, plus extra for brushing

Sea salt and freshly ground black pepper to taste

Baguette, cut into about 16 slices

1 Tbsp balsamic vinegar

1. Preheat the oven to 475°F.

2. In a medium bowl, mix together the tomatoes, garlic, fresh basil, red onion and black olives (if using), lemon juice, olive oil, and salt and pepper. Set aside. Toss occasionally while you prepare the bread.

3. Brush one side of each slice of bread with olive oil. Arrange on a baking sheet, and toast with the oiled side down for 5 to 7 minutes or until golden.

4. Top the toasted side of each bread slice with the room-temperature tomato mixture just before serving so the toast will stay crispy.

5. Drizzle several drops of balsamic vinegar over each piece of bruschetta before serving.

→   TIP The toasted slices can be made ahead and stored in an airtight container. Cool completely before storing.

Artichoke Spinach Dip

SERVES 8–12

Cheese lovers in my family can hardly wait for this dip to emerge from the oven.

....

One 8 oz package cream cheese, softened

¼ cup salad dressing (Miracle Whip or similar)

¼ cup grated Parmesan cheese

¼ cup grated Romano cheese

3 small cloves garlic, finely chopped

1 Tbsp chopped fresh basil

½ tsp garlic salt

14 oz can artichoke hearts, drained and chopped

1 cup chopped fresh spinach, or ½ cup frozen, drained

Sea salt and freshly ground black pepper to taste

¼ cup shredded mozzarella cheese

1. Preheat the oven to 350°F.

2. Lightly oil an 8- × 8-inch baking dish.

3. In a medium bowl, mix together the cream cheese, salad dressing, Parmesan cheese, Romano cheese, garlic, basil, and garlic salt.

4. Gently stir in the chopped artichoke hearts and spinach. Add salt and pepper to taste.

5. Transfer the mixture to the prepared baking dish. Top with mozzarella cheese.

6. Bake in the preheated oven for 25 minutes or until bubbly and lightly browned.

7. Serve hot with crusty bread or tortilla chips.

Devilled Eggs

YIELD: 12 EGG HALVES

This tasty high-protein dish is easy to prepare but will make you look like you are a seasoned chef. Serve it as an appetizer, a luncheon side dish, or a snack at a picnic.

6 large eggs, hard-boiled (see below)
2–3 Tbsp salad dressing (Miracle Whip or similar)
1 tsp sweet relish (such as hot dog relish)
½ tsp sea salt

¼ tsp freshly ground black pepper
¼ tsp dry mustard
½ tsp paprika or sprig of fresh parsley to garnish

1. Cut each egg lengthwise on a cutting board.

2. Use a small spoon or the tip of a small knife to remove the yolk. Place cooked yolks in a medium bowl.

3. Arrange the cooked egg whites on a platter.

4. Mash the yolks with a fork until smooth. Blend in the salad dressing, relish, salt, pepper, and dry mustard.

5. Carefully spoon approximately 1 Tbsp of the blended yolk mixture into each egg white until all is used.

6. Sprinkle each egg with paprika or top with a sprig of parsley.

→ **TIP** Transfer the yolk mixture into a small plastic bag with a snipped-off corner, or into a piping bag, and squeeze the yolk into the egg whites.

On the serving platter around the eggs, place sprigs of fresh parsley, cherry tomatoes, radishes, or sliced cucumber.

HOW TO HARD-BOIL AND PEEL EGGS

1. In a medium saucepan, add enough cold water to cover the eggs by 1 inch. Set the timer for 15 (to 20) minutes. Bring to a boil.

2. Simmer until the timer is up. Move the eggs around gently with a spoon during the first 5 minutes of cooking to make sure the yolks cook in the centre of the egg.

3. Remove from the heat and place the eggs in cold water for 5 to 10 minutes. Cold water creates a layer of steam between the shell and the egg white, which makes it easier to peel the egg. Older eggs are always easier to peel than farm-fresh eggs.

4. Hold each egg under cold running tap water, and crack the shell using the back of a spoon.

5. Gently slip the edge of the spoon under the membrane beneath the shell, following the curve of the egg and lifting off the shell.

6. Rinse the eggs thoroughly to remove any remaining bits of shell.

Easy Spinach Salad 12

Iceberg Lettuce Salad 13

Kale and Spinach Salad 15

Cabbage Salad 16

Egg Salad 17

Cauliflower Salad 18

Vickie's Tuna Salad 21

Wild Salmon Salad 22

Potato Salad 23

Boiled New Potatoes with Butter 24

Bill's Pan-Fried Potatoes 26

Creamy Garlic Whipped Potatoes 28

Vickie's Potato Chips 31

Oven-Roasted Herb Potatoes 33

Twice-Baked Potatoes 35

Quinoa Pilaf 36

Salads
AND
SIDES

Easy Spinach Salad

Protein, iron, and calcium in an appetizing combination that even youngsters love.

6–8 slices bacon

6 cups fresh spinach, stems removed, rinsed well

½ red onion, thinly sliced

½ tsp freshly ground black pepper

3 tsp balsamic vinegar

4–6 thin slices fresh bocconcini

3 eggs, hard-boiled (see page 8) and quartered

1. In a heavy skillet over medium-high heat, fry the bacon until crispy (5 to 7 minutes). Transfer the cooked bacon to a paper towel–lined plate. Crumble when cool.

2. Evenly fill 4 to 6 salad bowls with fresh spinach.

3. Wilt the spinach in each bowl in the microwave for 3 to 4 seconds.

4. Distribute the onion slices evenly over the spinach, and sprinkle with pepper and balsamic vinegar.

5. Top each bowl with a cheese slice, and garnish with the eggs and bacon.

Iceberg Lettuce Salad

SERVES 4

Serve alone or with meals in summer when iceberg lettuce is freshest.

2 Tbsp chopped pecans

2 Tbsp diced tomato

2 Tbsp diced onion

2 Tbsp raisins

2 Tbsp crumbled blue cheese

½ cup buttermilk

2 Tbsp salad dressing (Miracle Whip or similar)

½ tsp Worcestershire sauce

½ tsp hot sauce, like Sriracha

Juice of 1 lemon

1 head iceberg lettuce, quartered and core removed

1. In a medium bowl, mix the pecans, tomato, onion, and raisins.

2. In a separate bowl, mix the blue cheese, buttermilk, salad dressing, Worcestershire sauce, pepper sauce, and lemon juice. Add to the pecan mixture and coat evenly.

3. Place the quartered lettuce on individual plates, and pour the dressing overtop. Serve immediately.

→ TIP If you don't want to use buttermilk, you can replace it with kefir or use ½ cup yogurt mixed with 2 Tbsp water instead.

Kale and Spinach Salad

SERVES 4-6

This salad contains nutrient-rich raw kale and spinach. Sometimes kale can be tough. Marinating and massaging it by hand for a few minutes makes it tender.

1 Tbsp red wine vinegar

Juice of 1 lemon

2 Tbsp pure coconut oil or extra virgin olive oil

1 bunch curly leaf kale, washed, stems and veins removed, and cut into ½-inch ribbons

1 tsp sea salt

1 bunch fresh spinach, washed, stems removed, and cut into ½-inch ribbons

1 clove garlic, finely chopped or grated

2 Tbsp grated Parmesan cheese

½ cup chopped walnuts

½ cup chopped dried cranberries

1 tomato, finely chopped

Freshly ground black pepper to taste

1. In a small bowl, mix the vinegar, lemon juice, and oil. Massage the oil mixture into the kale leaves, then sprinkle the leaves with salt and rub it into the leaves. Allow to marinate for several minutes.

2. Add the spinach and garlic and toss.

3. Add the cheese, walnuts, cranberries, and tomato and toss lightly.

4. Grind fresh pepper onto the salad to taste, and serve.

Cabbage Salad

SERVES 4-6

My husband, Bill, absolutely LOVED this recipe, so I made it often. My mother-in-law always called it Cabbage Salad, not "coleslaw," so I do too! It's perfect to serve with fish and chicken. Raw cabbage is a healthy addition to any diet.

1 medium cabbage

3 green onions, cleaned and finely chopped

½ carrot, peeled and grated

2 Tbsp white vinegar

2 Tbsp granulated sugar

½ cup salad dressing (Miracle Whip or similar)

½ tsp sea salt, plus more to taste

1 tsp freshly ground black pepper, plus more to taste

Cherry tomatoes (optional)

1. Remove and discard the outer leaves and core of the cabbage.

2. Slice the cabbage into quarters. Chop the cabbage with a knife or use the large slot of a grater to produce uniformly sized pieces about ¼ inch wide.

3. Place the chopped cabbage in a large mixing bowl. Add the green onions and carrot.

4. In a separate medium bowl, combine the vinegar, sugar, and salad dressing (in that order so it won't curdle), and whisk until smooth and the sugar is completely dissolved.

5. Add the dressing to the cabbage. Mix completely.

6. Add salt and pepper.

7. Garnish with cherry tomatoes, if using.

→ TIP Don't use a food processor to chop the cabbage because it will produce too much cabbage juice and cause the salad to lose its crunchy texture.

Egg Salad

SERVES 3–4

This egg salad is delicious as a sandwich filling or scooped into a Boston lettuce (also know as butter lettuce) leaf.

6 eggs, hard-boiled

About 2 Tbsp salad dressing (Miracle Whip or similar)

¼ cup diced celery

¼ cup finely chopped green onions

1 tsp sweet relish (such as hot dog relish)

Sea salt and freshly ground black pepper to taste

Bread-and-butter pickles (optional)

1. Peel the eggs and rinse under tap water to ensure all bits of shell are removed. (For tips, see page 8.)

2. In a large bowl, mash the eggs well with a potato masher or the back of a fork.

3. Add enough salad dressing to make a spread. Add celery, green onions, and sweet relish.

4. Add salt and pepper to taste. Use immediately as a sandwich spread or scooped into Boston lettuce leaves. Garnish with bread-and-butter pickles if using. Unused egg salad can be covered tightly and refrigerated for up to 24 hours.

Cauliflower Salad

SERVES 4

Almost any vegetable can be turned into an appetizing salad by marinating it in vinaigrette. A steamer basket is a quick, easy, and healthy way to cook vegetables.

2 cups small cauliflower florets

1 Tbsp extra virgin olive oil

1 Tbsp orange juice

½ tsp orange zest

1 ½ tsp white wine vinegar or white vinegar

¼ cup finely chopped fresh parsley

1. In a covered medium-size pan using a steamer basket, steam the cauliflower over medium-high heat. Cook for about 4 minutes or until tender. If you don't have a steamer basket, use a covered 12-inch skillet to cook the cauliflower for 3 or 4 minutes in an inch of boiling water.

2. Drain the cooked cauliflower, and rinse under cold water to stop the cooking process. Drain again and set aside.

3. In a medium bowl, combine the oil, orange juice, and orange zest.

4. Add the cooked cauliflower and toss gently.

5. Cover and refrigerate for 2 to 3 hours, tossing occasionally.

6. Add the vinegar and parsley just before serving and toss well.

VARIATION

Instead of cauliflower, steam 1 ½ lb asparagus for 4 minutes or until tender. For the vinaigrette, combine 2 ½ tsp extra virgin olive oil, 1 Tbsp finely chopped green onion, ½ tsp spicy brown mustard, and 1 ½ tsp white wine vinegar. Toss the asparagus in the dressing, cover, and refrigerate for 2 to 3 hours.

Shown here with Cabbage Salad (see page 16) ›

Vickie's Tuna Salad

SERVES 4-6

This salad is always a welcome addition to any barbecue, potluck, or luncheon. My family loves yellowfin tuna, so it's what I use in this recipe, but you can substitute any canned tuna. Add some Sriracha sauce to spice things up!

2 cups elbow macaroni

Two 6 oz cans yellowfin tuna, drained

½ cup green peas, fresh or frozen, cooked

1 cup chopped green onions

2 stalks celery, finely chopped

½ cup salad dressing (Miracle Whip or similar)

Sea salt and freshly ground black pepper to taste

1. In a large pot of boiling water, add the macaroni and cook until tender, about 12 to 15 minutes. Drain and cool.

2. Mix the macaroni, tuna, peas, green onions, and celery together in a large mixing bowl. Fold in the salad dressing and coat the ingredients evenly. Add salt and pepper to taste.

3. Cover and refrigerate for 2 to 3 hours before serving.

Boiled New Potatoes with Butter

SERVES 2-4

New potatoes are my favourite potato dish. On the farm in summer, potato plants in bloom in the field meant that the little potatoes were just starting to "set" underground. Bill would check on what the future yield might be by pulling up the plants to count the potatoes under them. Then he'd put the potatoes back in the ground to wait for them to grow bigger. Potatoes are sold by weight, and in our business we were paid by the hundredweight (each burlap bag weighing a hundred pounds). We needed every potato to grow as large as possible under the ground. Every single potato counted in order to pay back the bank loan in the fall.

One summer afternoon, Bill was out checking the potato fields. That day he didn't have a bag or box handy, I guess, and he showed up in our farm kitchen in his socks, workboots in hand. He smiled at me and shyly presented his size-eleven boots. I looked inside the boots and saw they were filled with tiny, delicate new potatoes just for me! At that moment I knew I was accepting the most unique and tender token of his love for me. That is just one of the special memories I cherish from our busy years together on our potato farm.

One year, Bill planted two acres of early potatoes for me next to the farmhouse so I could easily dig them up between other chores and the demands of our small children. You might think by now that I was going to eat all those little new potatoes myself. But here's what I planned to do. I'd eat some and sell the rest. We needed income during the summer while our potato crop was maturing underground, so I had the idea of selling new potatoes at our farm door. I figured that, if I loved them so much, there might be other people with a taste like mine who would pay a little extra. At first I was shy about meeting customers, but we needed that income, and with time I learned that marketing my potatoes to potato lovers like me was fun!

I'd harvest the little potatoes by hand or carefully dig them with a potato fork in July, when they were still very small and the skins were hardly set. I dug only the amount I projected to sell each day to make sure they were fresh for my customers. I was careful not to rub their delicate skins while I filled twelve-quart wooden baskets with them. I believed presentation was very important. I made a New Potatoes for Sale sign for the end of our laneway, but my potato sales were slow at the farmhouse, so I decided to go to a location where there was some traffic. After a short drive down the highway, I found a spot on the side of the road to set up shop.

I recall being this dusty gal straight out of the field (but with great tan lines!). I sold my new potatoes out of the back of our old green F-150. Anyone who stopped on Simcoe County Road en route to Collingwood or Wasaga Beach, Ontario, to buy potatoes during the 1980s most definitely bought new potatoes from me!

. . . .

20 very small new potatoes with skins, washed

1. In a pot of boiling water, cook the potatoes until almost tender, about 8 to 10 minutes. Don't overcook. Drain and serve with butter.

Bill's Pan-Fried Potatoes

SERVES 2

Leftover potatoes were always useful in the farm kitchen. I never worried about making too many potatoes for supper because they would be great for a quick meal any time the next day. They go perfectly with eggs, steak, or canned salmon sprinkled with a bit of vinegar.

I remember the first time Bill cooked supper for me. I was visiting the Kerr farmhouse where his parents lived. He impressed me with his domestic skills that night by serving me a meal of scrambled eggs and fried potatoes.

1 Tbsp extra virgin olive oil or butter
3 cups thinly sliced or diced boiled potatoes
Sea salt and freshly ground black pepper to taste

1. Heat the oil or butter in a heavy skillet on medium-high.

2. Add the potatoes and turn them over often until heated through and crispy on the outside.

3. Season to taste with salt and pepper, and serve.

Vickie's Potato Chips

SERVES 2

The first time I made a small batch of these chips for Bill and our four children using the potatoes we grew, I ate almost the whole thing myself—still warm. They tasted that good, even with no salt.

. . . .

6 medium potatoes, unpeeled and scrubbed
2 cups pure peanut oil
Sea salt to taste

1. Thinly slice the potatoes on a cutting board with a sharp knife. The slice should be thicker than what a commercial slicer produces. Try to create a uniform slice thickness so the potato chips cook evenly and completely.

2. In a heavy pot, heat the oil to 375°F–380°F. Continually check the temperature with a cooking thermometer.

3. Drop one potato slice into the hot oil. If the slice begins to cook rapidly, bubbling around the edges, the oil is hot enough. If the oil temperature is too low, the potato slice will absorb the oil.

4. Carefully add 1 cup of potato slices to the oil. Stir gently to prevent the slices from sticking together. Cook until golden.

5. Remove the chips from the oil with a slotted spoon, and drain on a paper towel. Sprinkle with sea salt while still warm. Continue cooking small batches until all potatoes are cooked.

6. Serve warm or cooled.

→ TIP Make sure to find the right type of potato for your chips. There are many different varieties of potatoes. Some are grown for table use—boiling, baking, or frying—while others are grown specifically for food processing. Chip-stock potatoes are low in sugar content and high in dry matter. They are grown to produce "white" potato chips.

Chip potatoes aren't normally found in the supermarket unless a chip-stock grower has an oversupply. Early crop potatoes, like those in spring and summer, will usually cook to a light golden colour. Unless you prefer dark potato chips, don't purchase potatoes with yellow or gold-coloured flesh to make potato chips. Try using a baking potato, like a russet, instead.

Oven-Roasted Herb Potatoes

SERVES 4–6

Preparing my oven-roasted potato recipe takes extra time and attention, but the resulting taste and texture are worth it. I prefer to roast partially cooked (parboiled) potatoes in coconut or peanut oil in a separate pan in the oven even if I'm cooking a roast. This produces a light-tasting, "crispy on the outside and fluffy on the inside" potato without the taste of the roast. You may substitute your favourite herbs for any used in this recipe.

· ·

10 medium potatoes (like russets), peeled and cut in quarters or sixths

¼ cup pure coconut or peanut oil, plus more for oiling pan

1 Tbsp chopped fresh rosemary

1 Tbsp chopped fresh Italian parsley

1 tsp chopped fresh tarragon

1 tsp freshly ground black pepper

1. Generously oil a large baking pan and set aside.

2. Bring a large pot of water to a boil. Cook the potatoes on medium-high heat for about 10 minutes, until partially cooked. The potatoes should be slightly firm and hold their shape.

3. Drain and transfer the potatoes to a colander to dry and cool slightly.

4. In a small bowl, mix the oil together with the rosemary, parsley, tarragon, and pepper.

5. Heat the oiled baking pan in a preheated oven at 425°F for 5 minutes. Carefully remove the pan from the oven, and arrange the potatoes in a single layer.

6. Brush the oil-herb mixture all over the potatoes with a pastry brush, and bake on the middle rack of the oven for 10 minutes.

7. Remove the pan from the oven to turn the potatoes over, checking that each side is golden brown before turning and that there is oil on all sides of each potato. Continue to bake until all sides are light brown.

8. Set the oven to broil. Watch the potatoes carefully, turning them every 5 minutes or so until they are golden brown and crisp on all sides, about 10 to 15 minutes. Serve immediately.

→ TIP Sometimes it's convenient to add parboiled potatoes to a pan of roasting meat instead of cooking them on their own. For a heartier flavour, use pan drippings to coat the potatoes while the roast is still in the oven. Arrange the potatoes around the roast during the last hour of cooking. Use oven mitts and a long-handled spatula to carefully turn the potatoes while roasting.

Twice-Baked Potatoes

SERVES 4

This is the perfect side dish with steak or seafood or is a delicious snack on its own.

4 large baking potatoes

1 ¼ cups shredded sharp cheddar cheese, divided

4 green onions, finely chopped, divided

1 cup sour cream

3 bacon slices, cooked crispy and crumbled

1. Preheat the oven to 400°F.

2. Scrub the potatoes and pierce them with a fork twice to prevent them from exploding in the oven while baking.

3. Space the potatoes apart on the middle oven rack, and bake until they are soft all the way through when pierced with a fork, approximately 50 minutes.

4. While the potatoes are baking, in a medium bowl, fold 1 cup cheese and three-quarters of the chopped green onions into the sour cream. Cover and place in the refrigerator until the potatoes are cooked. Set aside the remaining cheese and onions.

5. Transfer the baked potatoes to a cutting board. Leave the oven on.

6. When the potatoes are cool enough to handle, slit them lengthwise across the top, cutting only enough so that you can remove the potato inside but not slicing all the way through. Being careful not to tear the skins, scoop the insides of the baked potatoes out and transfer to a large bowl. Mash the cooked potatoes with a fork until smooth. Add the sour cream mixture and blend well. Using a small spoon, stuff the potato skins with this mixture.

7. Return the stuffed potatoes to the hot oven and bake for 10 minutes.

8. After baking, sprinkle the crumbled bacon and the remaining cheese and green onions on top of the potatoes.

9. Serve immediately or cool, wrap tightly, and refrigerate for up to 2 days.

Quinoa Pilaf

SERVES 6

One of the world's true super foods, quinoa is a complete protein, containing all nine essential amino acids. Quinoa is a great source of fibre, iron, and magnesium. This light and wholesome grain can be prepared quickly and easily with this basic method.

2 cups quinoa, rinsed

4 cups filtered water

½ cup diced carrots

½ cup finely chopped green onions

¼ cup diced celery

¼ cup diced green pepper

¼ cup diced sweet red pepper

¼ cup extra virgin olive oil

2 cloves garlic, crushed

¼ tsp dried thyme leaves

Sea salt to taste

1. Place the quinoa and water in a medium saucepan and bring to a boil. Reduce the heat and simmer, covered, until all the water is absorbed, about 15 minutes.

2. In a large skillet, sauté the vegetables and garlic in the olive oil for 3 to 5 minutes. Stir in the thyme.

3. Add to the cooked quinoa, mixing well.

4. Add salt to taste.

→ TIP Quinoa pilaf is delicious served as a side dish with fish and can be used as a stuffing for a red pepper. Vary the pilaf using your favourite vegetables or by cooking the quinoa in chicken, fish, or vegetable stock instead of water.

Chicken Stock 40

Vegetable Soup 41

French Onion Soup 42

French Canadian Pea Soup 45

Irish Canadian Beef Stew 46

Kowalski Cabbage Rolls 49

Shepherd's Pie 50

Macaroni and Beef Casserole 52

Soups, Stews, AND CASSEROLES

Chicken Stock

YIELD: 6 CUPS

Use this stock as a base for soups, add it to stews, or just drink it as is when you have a cold.

....

Leftover carcass from a roasted chicken

4 carrots, peeled and cut to fit pot

2 stalks celery, cut to fit pot

2 large onions, peeled and quartered

2 bay leaves

1 tsp dried thyme leaves

Sea salt and freshly ground
   black pepper to taste

1. Place the roast chicken carcass and vegetables in a large stockpot, cover with cold filtered water, and bring to a boil.

2. Add the herbs and salt and pepper.

3. Cover and simmer on the stovetop for about 3 hours. Add more water if needed to cover the ingredients.

4. After 3 hours, allow some of the water to boil off, reducing the stock to provide a richer flavour.

5. Cool. Pour through a mesh strainer to remove the vegetables and herbs.

6. Transfer the chicken stock to glass canning jars, and refrigerate for up to a week or freeze for up to a month for later use in a soup recipe.

SLOW COOKER VERSION

In a slow cooker, bring all the ingredients to a boil. Cook for 3 hours on low heat, then take the lid off the slow cooker, set to high heat, and continue to cook until the broth is reduced. This provides a richer flavour.

→ **TIP** To freeze, pour the cooled stock into a sanitized canning jar, and leave space at the top to allow for expansion so the glass won't crack. If you don't have jars handy, use food-quality 1-gallon freezer bags, and lay them flat while they freeze to take up less space.

Vegetable Soup

Healthy and delicious, this soup is one of my favourite slow cooker meals.
Enjoy your veggies!

. . . .

½ medium cabbage, diced

3 small zucchini, washed and diced

2 cups chopped fresh spinach

1 cup sliced carrots

1 onion, chopped (optional)

2 potatoes, diced (optional)

1 large clove garlic, finely chopped

1 tsp chopped fresh basil

½ tsp freshly ground black pepper

Sea salt to taste

4 cups Chicken Stock (see facing page)

14 oz can diced tomatoes

2 Tbsp tomato paste

Dash of Worcestershire sauce

1. In a large pot on medium-low heat, combine all ingredients and add enough filtered water to cover the ingredients. Cook until the vegetables are tender, approximately 30 to 40 minutes.

SLOW COOKER VERSION
Combine all the ingredients, cover with water, and cook on the low setting for 3 to 6 hours.

French Onion Soup

SERVES 4

French onion soup is a classic Quebec favourite. My recipe makes it easy to whip up this authentic gourmet dish at home. Ovenproof bowls are required to bake the soup in the oven the traditional way, topped with Gruyère cheese.

....

3 large sweet white or yellow onions

3 Tbsp butter

1 tsp extra virgin olive oil

½ tsp granulated sugar

1 tsp sea salt, plus more to taste

1 tsp freshly ground black pepper, plus more to taste

1 tsp unbleached all-purpose flour

4 cups beef stock (low-sodium)

1 cup dry white or red wine

4 baguette slices, 1½–2 inches thick

Softened butter for the baguette slices

½ lb Gruyère cheese, shredded (about 2 cups)

1. Peel and chop the onions into ½-inch pieces.

2. Melt the butter and oil in a large, heavy skillet over medium-low heat. Add the onions to the skillet. Increase to medium-high heat for 2 minutes, then cover and reduce the heat to low. Cook slowly, stirring occasionally, until the onions are soft and translucent, about 20 minutes.

3. Remove the cover. Increase the heat to medium-high. Add the sugar, salt, and pepper. Continue to cook, stirring, until the onions are very soft and a deep, golden brown, about 20 to 30 minutes.

4. Reduce the heat to medium, sprinkle the flour over the onions, and stir constantly for 2 to 3 minutes.

5. Add 1 cup of the stock and blend well. Add the remaining 3 cups of stock and stir. Add the wine and continue to stir. Season to taste with salt and pepper and reduce the heat. Simmer for 25 to 30 minutes.

6. Preheat the oven to 425°F.

7. Remove the crusts from the slices of baguette, if preferred. Butter both sides, then toast in the oven until golden brown on both sides (3 to 5 minutes per side). Keep the oven on.

8. Place a slice of toasted bread at the bottom of each of 4 ovenproof bowls, and fill the bowls with the onion soup.

9. Sprinkle a thick layer of shredded Gruyère cheese on top of the soup. Arrange the bowls on a baking sheet to prevent spills in the oven. Bake until the cheese has melted and is bubbly and light brown, about 15 minutes.

10. Broil for an additional 5 minutes until the cheese is bubbling, being careful not to burn the cheese. Remove from the oven and cool for 5 minutes before serving.

→ **TIP** Use red wine instead of white for a richer-tasting soup. You can also place the toasted bread on top of the soup and cover with cheese if preferred. Substitute mozzarella cheese for the Gruyère—it's good, but not quite as tasty!

French Canadian Pea Soup

YIELD: 6-8 CUPS

This traditional recipe from Quebec calls for yellow split peas and salt pork. I use a ham bone and serve the soup with a loaf of crusty bread.

Savory is the secret spice that produces a soup with the exact aroma and flavour I remember as a child on a snowy winter day in Montreal. My own children grew up eating this soup on the farm, and as adults they still love the taste of it when the weather gets chilly. They claim my homemade version of this *habitants*-style soup is better than soup from any can.

. . . .

1 lb dried yellow split peas (about 2 cups)

8 cups cold filtered water

1 ham bone

1 large onion, finely chopped

½ cup finely chopped celery

¼ cup grated carrot

½ tsp dried savory

1 tsp sea salt, plus more to taste

½ tsp freshly ground black pepper,
    plus more to taste

1. Sort and rinse the yellow peas in cold water, discarding any that are blemished or discoloured. Place in a large pot of cold water.

2. Add the ham bone, onion, celery, carrot, savory, salt, and pepper. Bring to a boil; skim and discard any foam that rises to the surface.

3. Reduce the heat and simmer until the peas are very tender, about 2 to 4 hours. Add more water as needed to keep the peas covered at all times. Stir occasionally to prevent scorching. You can also transfer the soup to a slow cooker and cook on low for 6 to 8 hours.

4. Remove the ham bone and scrape the meat from the bone. Chop the meat and return it to the soup.

5. Season to taste with sea salt and pepper.

→ TIP For a thicker soup, purée 1 cup of cooked soup in a blender and return it to the pot. The soup will also thicken after refrigeration, so if you wish to thin it down again, add a little water and reheat it before serving.

This soup can be made with the leftovers from a baked ham dinner. Just freeze the ham bone with some meat left on for up to a month to use in this soup recipe. It is also possible to purchase only the ham bone from the butcher if you don't mind not having chunks of ham in the soup.

Irish Canadian Beef Stew

SERVES 6

Traditionally, this hearty peasant meal was made with lamb and root vegetables in Ireland. I used beef in my recipe because my freezer was full of it! It's easy to prepare on the stovetop, but now I use a slow cooker for a nutritious and satisfying meal that can be left unattended almost all day. Throw all the ingredients into the slow cooker in the morning and the stew will be ready by dinner.

½ cup rice flour

¼ tsp sea salt

1 tsp freshly ground black pepper

1 ½ lb stewing beef, trimmed of fat and cubed

1 ½ Tbsp extra virgin olive oil

½ cup red wine, divided

3 cups beef stock, divided

½ tsp Worcestershire sauce

About ½ cup filtered water

1 large yellow onion, chopped

4 medium potatoes, peeled or unpeeled and quartered

4 medium carrots, scraped and chopped

1 small turnip (optional), peeled and finely chopped

1 stalk celery with leaves, chopped

2 cloves garlic, finely chopped

1 bay leaf

½ tsp dried thyme leaves

Sea salt and freshly ground black pepper to taste

3 Tbsp butter

¼ cup unbleached all-purpose flour

1. Combine the rice flour, salt, and pepper on a plate. Coat each cube of meat in the flour mixture on all sides.

2. Heat the oil in a heavy skillet on medium-high. Place all meat cubes into the hot oil.

3. Keeping the heat high enough to sear but not burn the meat, brown the meat on all sides, using tongs to turn the meat, about 3 to 5 minutes in total. Place the browned meat in a large pot or a heated slow cooker.

4. Pour ¼ cup of the wine and ¼ cup of the stock to cover the bottom of the skillet. Bring to a boil and scrape the pan to deglaze. Pour this liquid over the meat, then add the remaining wine and stock, the Worcestershire sauce, and enough water to cover the meat.

5. Add the vegetables, garlic, bay leaf, thyme, and salt and pepper.

6. Cover and cook on the stovetop on medium-low heat for 2 to 3 hours, or in a slow cooker on low for 6 to 8 hours, until the meat is tender when pierced with a fork.

7. To thicken the stew, create a roux by melting the butter in a skillet, then adding the flour. Bring to a boil. Reduce the heat to a simmer and cook until golden brown, whisking constantly to combine.

8. Just before serving, add the roux to the hot stew, stirring evenly with a mixing spoon, and bring to a boil. Slice the quartered potatoes into smaller pieces.

→ **TIP** Add 2 Tbsp tomato paste and ¼ cup barley with the vegetables for a thicker, richer stew.

Kowalski Cabbage Rolls

YIELD: 16–18 ROLLS

This recipe is from Bill's mother's family. They immigrated to Canada from Poland at the turn of the last century and settled near Alliston, Ontario.

1 large green cabbage

1 large onion, chopped

1 ½ Tbsp extra virgin olive oil

1 ½ lb ground pork

½ lb ground beef

1 ½ cups cooked long-grain rice

1 tsp finely chopped garlic

1 tsp sea salt, plus more to taste

¼ tsp freshly ground black pepper, plus more to taste

2 cans condensed tomato soup

½ cup filtered water

1 cup sour cream

1. Remove the core and outer leaves from the cabbage. Place the whole head in a stockpot half-filled with boiling salted water. Cover and cook for 10 to 15 minutes or until the leaves are soft. Remove the cabbage from the water, and check to make sure the thick part of the leaf is soft. When the leaves are cool enough to handle, remove one at a time and set 16 to 18 leaves aside. Chop the remaining cabbage and place it in the bottom of a 9-x 13-inch casserole or baking dish with at least 3-inch sides.

2. In a large frying pan, sauté the chopped onion in olive oil until tender and translucent. Transfer to a large bowl with a slotted spoon to cool slightly.

3. Add the pork, beef, rice, garlic, salt, and pepper to the onions and mix well.

4. Preheat the oven to 350°F. Using a paring knife, shave down the thick centre stem on each cabbage leaf so that the leaf has an even thickness. Take care not to cut all the way through.

5. Place about ½ cup of the meat mixture on each leaf. Roll away from you to encase the meat. Fold the sides of the leaf toward the centre and continue to roll away from you to create a neat little package.

6. Place the cabbage rolls in the casserole dish on top of the chopped cabbage. Arrange so that the loose edge of the leaf is at the bottom. Season with salt and pepper.

7. Mix the soup and water and pour evenly over the rolls.

8. Bake, uncovered, for 1 hour or until the cabbage is very tender. Baste often with the tomato soup during baking to prevent the cabbage rolls from drying out.

9. Serve with the pan juices and a drizzle of sour cream, or mix the sour cream with the pan juices and ladle it over the cabbage rolls.

→ **TIP** Cabbage rolls freeze well for up to 2 weeks before or after cooking.

If you use a slow cooker instead of the oven, cook the cabbage rolls on low for about 6 hours, then transfer to a casserole dish and bake in the oven for 15 minutes, basting with soup until the tops are browned.

Shepherd's Pie

SERVES 6

This traditional comfort food can be served piping hot from the oven on a cold winter evening or warmed up the next day. When I was growing up in Quebec, this recipe was a filling and thrifty meal for a large family. Serve with Pickled Beets (see page 120), Iceberg Lettuce Salad (see page 13), and warm crusty bread.

. . . .

6-8 medium potatoes, peeled and quartered
1 Tbsp butter, plus more for dotting on the crust
About ¼ cup whole milk
1 Tbsp extra virgin olive oil
1 yellow or Spanish onion, diced

2 lb ground beef
1 tsp sea salt
1 Tbsp freshly ground black pepper
Two 15 oz cans creamed sweet corn

1. Add the potatoes to a pot of boiling water and cook on medium-high until tender, about 20 minutes. Drain.

2. Mash the hot potatoes with a potato masher. Add butter and some of the milk and mash again. Beat with an electric mixer, adding just enough milk to whip the potatoes until they're fluffy. Cover to keep warm and set aside.

3. In a heavy skillet on medium, heat the oil and sauté the onions for 3 to 4 minutes. Transfer the onions to a large mixing bowl and set aside.

4. Using the same skillet, cook the ground beef with the salt and pepper on medium-high heat until no longer pink, crumbling the beef with a fork as it cooks.

5. Transfer the beef to the onion bowl using a slotted spoon to drain off any fat. Mix well.

6. Preheat the oven to 400°F.

7. Line the bottom of a 7- × 11-inch baking or casserole dish with the meat and onion mixture. Pour the creamed corn over the meat.

8. Spread the whipped potatoes evenly on top of the corn, right to the edges of the casserole dish, to form a crust. Use a spatula to make peaks on the potato crust for a decorative look. Dot with butter.

9. Bake, uncovered, until the potatoes are golden brown, about 30 minutes.

10. Broil for an additional 5 to 7 minutes, browning but not burning the top.

11. Remove from the oven, cover, and allow the casserole to set for 5 to 10 minutes before serving.

→ **TIP** Place a baking sheet under the casserole dish to catch any spills.

Macaroni and Beef Casserole

SERVES 4–6

Mary Kerr made a variation of this dish in her kitchen, and she passed it down to me with her blessing.

1 cup macaroni

1 large onion, chopped

1 Tbsp extra virgin olive oil

1 lb ground beef

28 oz can diced tomatoes

Sea salt and freshly ground
black pepper to taste

2 cups shredded cheddar cheese (optional)

1. Preheat the oven to 350°F. Oil a 9- × 13-inch casserole dish (or individual ovenproof dishes).

2. In a heavy pot, bring about 4 cups water to a boil. Add the macaroni and a pinch of salt and cook on medium heat for about 10 minutes or until al dente (slightly firm to the bite). Take care not to overcook.

3. While the macaroni is cooking, prepare the onions and ground beef. In a heavy skillet over medium-high heat, sauté the onions in hot oil for 3 to 5 minutes until transparent. Transfer the onions to the casserole dish.

4. In the same skillet, cook the meat on medium-high heat until no pink is visible. Transfer the meat to the casserole dish using a slotted spoon to drain off any fat.

5. Drain the cooked macaroni and transfer to the casserole dish.

6. Add the tomatoes to the macaroni and beef and mix well. Add salt and pepper to taste. Layer the top with cheddar, if using.

7. Bake, uncovered, at 350°F for 40 minutes or until bubbly around the edges.

Meatloaf 56

Spaghetti Sauce 57

Corned Beef and Cabbage 58

Prime Rib au Jus 60

Montreal Dry Garlic Spareribs 62

Chicken Kiev 65

Roast Chicken and Gravy 66

Apple-Stuffed Pork Loin Roast 68

Baked Wild Salmon 69

Fish and Chips 71

Shrimp Tacos 73

Meat
AND
SEAFOOD

Meatloaf

Start preparing this moist meatloaf about an hour and a half to two hours before you wish to eat, and serve it hot. It's also great cold and sliced for sandwiches.

1 cup whole milk

3 slices bread

1 ½ lb ground beef

1 cup grated Parmesan cheese

¼ tsp garlic powder

¾ tsp sea salt

½ tsp freshly ground black pepper

⅓ cup finely chopped fresh Italian parsley

3 eggs, beaten

½ cup tomato paste

½ cup filtered water

2 Tbsp vinegar

⅓ cup packed brown sugar

1 tsp dry mustard

Hot sauce, like Sriracha, to taste

Chopped fresh parsley for garnish

1. Preheat the oven to 350°F.

2. In a large bowl, pour the milk over the bread slices. Soak for several minutes.

3. Mix in the ground beef, milk-soaked bread, Parmesan, garlic powder, salt, pepper, and parsley. Add the beaten eggs. Mix all these ingredients with clean hands until well combined.

4. Transfer the mixture to a 9- × 5-inch loaf pan.

5. In a mixing bowl, combine the tomato paste, water, vinegar, brown sugar, mustard, and hot sauce.

6. Pour half of the mixture over the top of the beef. Spread evenly with a spoon and bake in the preheated oven for 45 to 50 minutes.

7. Spread the remaining sauce over the top of the loaf, and bake for an additional 15 to 20 minutes or until a meat thermometer inserted into the centre of the loaf reads 160°F.

8. Remove from the oven, cover with aluminum foil, and allow the loaf to rest for 10 minutes before slicing.

9. Garnish with fresh parsley, to serve.

→ TIP This meatloaf is great served with Kale and Spinach Salad (see page 15).

Spaghetti Sauce

SERVES 6–8

Preparing spaghetti sauce any day of the week is pure joy! I love the aroma of garlic cooking. I keep some red wine handy when I make this recipe. It's an ingredient in my sauce and for me to enjoy while I cook. I usually double this recipe and freeze some sauce for later. Tripling this recipe feeds about twenty guests, easily.

1 Tbsp extra virgin olive oil

2 cups chopped celery

1 medium onion, chopped

1 medium green pepper, chopped

28 oz can crushed or diced tomatoes

14 ½ oz can tomato sauce

4 oz can tomato paste

½ cup dry red wine

2 cloves garlic, finely chopped

½ tsp dried oregano

1 large fresh basil leaf, chopped

½ tsp dried thyme leaves

1 bay leaf

1 ½ lb ground beef

½ tsp garlic powder

Sea salt and freshly ground black pepper to taste

1. Heat the oil in a large skillet on medium. Sauté the celery, onion, and green pepper for 5 to 7 minutes. Set aside.

2. In a large, heavy saucepot or slow cooker on low heat, simmer the tomatoes, tomato sauce, and tomato paste with the wine. Add the garlic, oregano, basil, thyme, and bay leaf. Transfer the onion, celery, and pepper mixture to the tomato sauce and continue to simmer.

3. In a large skillet on medium heat, cook the ground beef with the garlic powder, stirring until the meat has lost its pink colour.

4. Use a slotted spoon to remove the beef from the fat. Add the beef to the tomato sauce.

5. Simmer on the stovetop for about 3 hours, stirring often to prevent the sauce from scorching on the bottom of the pot. You can also simmer in a slow cooker set on low heat for 4 to 6 hours. Add more water if the sauce becomes too thick.

6. Add salt and pepper to taste.

Corned Beef and Cabbage

SERVES 4–6

This traditional Irish dish is served on St. Patrick's Day. You can brine your own brisket and make corned beef yourself. It's easy and fun, and it tastes great! A few weeks beforehand, buy the beef brisket cut in the supermarket. Allow seven days to marinate the brisket in your refrigerator, then cook it as below using a slow cooker or in a pot on the stovetop.

BRINE

6 cups cold filtered water

¼ cup pickling salt

1 tsp freshly ground black pepper

2 tsp ground ginger

1 tsp ground cloves

2 bay leaves

1 Tbsp brown sugar

¼ tsp ground nutmeg

¼ tsp paprika

4 tsp finely chopped garlic

1 Tbsp potassium nitrate,
    dissolved in ½ cup warm water (see Tip)

4 lb beef brisket

COOKED BEEF

4 cups hot filtered water

2 Tbsp cider vinegar

2 Tbsp brown sugar

½ tsp freshly ground black pepper

¼ tsp paprika

1 large onion, cut into wedges

4 medium potatoes, scrubbed and diced

3 carrots, sliced

1 cabbage, cored and sliced or cut into 12 wedges

1. To prepare the brine, in a large, heavy pot, bring the cold water, pickling salt, pepper, ginger, cloves, bay leaves, brown sugar, nutmeg, paprika, garlic, and potassium nitrate to a boil. Remove from the heat and cool to room temperature.

2. Place the raw beef brisket in a large, strong, food-quality storage bag and cover with the cooled brine.

3. Leave in the refrigerator for 7 days, turning the bag over daily.

4. When you're ready to cook the beef, remove the beef from the brine.

5. In a large, preheated slow cooker on high or in a pot on the stove, combine the hot water, vinegar, brown sugar, pepper, paprika, and onion wedges.

6. Once the mixture is hot, transfer the beef to the slow cooker or pot. Arrange the potatoes and carrots alongside and on top of the beef.

7. Cover and cook in a slow cooker on high for 4 to 6 hours or simmer on the stovetop for 45 to 50 minutes, or until the beef is tender when pierced with a fork.

8. Remove the lid and arrange the cabbage over the top of the beef. Cover and continue cooking for 1 hour in the slow cooker or 20 minutes on the stovetop.

9. Transfer to a platter and slice.

10. Serve with the cabbage, carrots, potatoes, and some of the cooking liquid.

→ TIP Potassium nitrate can be purchased from a pharmacy. It keeps the meat pink during brining and cooking.

Prime Rib au Jus

SERVES 4–6

This recipe is foolproof and delicious. Our family gathers to celebrate Christmas Eve with this feast!

. . . .

6–8 lb prime rib beef, 2 to 3 bones
Sea salt and freshly ground black pepper to taste
1 ½ cups red wine

2 cups beef stock
1 tsp creamy horseradish

1. Bring the beef to room temperature.

2. Preheat the oven to 500°F.

3. Rub the beef with salt and pepper. Place in a roasting pan, bone side down.

4. Roast in the preheated oven for 30 minutes. Reduce the heat to 350°F and roast for 1 ½ hours more, or until a meat thermometer inserted in the centre of the roast reads 120°F.

5. Remove from the oven. Cover with aluminum foil and allow the roast to rest for 15 minutes while preparing the jus.

6. Add the wine and beef stock to the beef drippings in the roasting pan. Simmer over medium-low heat, whisking occasionally. Reduce to about half of the original volume. Add the horseradish to the jus and salt and pepper to taste.

7. Slice the roast beef and serve with the jus as a dip.

MEAT AND POTATOES

Every farmwife I knew in our area kept at least one deep freezer down in her basement. Some families owned two! A deep freezer was essential for storing vegetables, berries, and other fruit, but mainly we needed it for meat. Meat was the main ingredient in meals on our farm because Bill just loved it. I used to buy meat in a plastic tray at the grocery market, but that changed after I moved to the farm.

I learned all about beef without really wanting or trying to. A steer is a young bull that has been castrated and fed a special diet to produce muscle; steers are sold "on the hoof" by weight at auction sales. The "dressed price" was the price we paid for the final weight of meat we would take home. I didn't ask what happened to the rest of the animal, but I expect it was used in some appropriate manner.

The first time I split a steer with my sister-in-law, Corinne, we bought it from Bill's oldest sister, Isabel. She and her husband raised cattle and pigs on their farm near Cookstown, Ontario, and we bought our steer right from the farm just before it went to market. After it was killed, it had to hang for the prerequisite number of days at the abattoir (slaughterhouse) so the meat could age. Aging the meat made it tender.

We made an appointment to visit the butcher there to tell him how we each wanted him to cut our half. Did we want big roasts? More prime rib or T-bone steaks? Rump or round roasts or round steaks? Did we want some ground beef? How many pounds per package? All these questions confounded me my first time there. I just guessed and tried to sound like I actually knew what I wanted.

Huddled in wool sweaters in the chilly shop, Corinne and I could hear the electric meat-saw tearing through bones as the butcher cut our meat to order. He wrapped our individual packages and transferred them to his walk-in deep freezer because it would be much faster than freezing the hundreds of pounds of meat at home. That would have taken days! We returned the next day to pick up our boxes of frozen meat, neatly labelled and organized, ready to be transferred to our farmhouse freezers.

I never bought beef from the supermarket again. I can't explain exactly why, but with our freezer filled with all that meat, on some level I felt that we were exceedingly rich!

Sometimes farmers traded commodities between each other with no money exchanged. My neighbour raised roasting chickens, and she would regularly deliver a few birds to me (cleaned and with the feathers already plucked, thank goodness!). Our family really enjoyed a fresh roasted chicken for Sunday dinner. We traded potatoes for them at first, but after we began making potato chips, this neighbour always preferred to trade her chickens for Miss Vickie's chips.

Montreal Dry Garlic Spareribs

SERVES 2-4

Simmering ribs in this unique sauce is the secret to this delectable Montreal specialty. The recipe is easy to prepare at home. Ask your butcher to cut a slab of regular spareribs in half or thirds if you prefer to make smaller ribs.

. . . .

½ onion, cut in wedges

1 bay leaf

½ tsp sea salt

1 tsp freshly ground black pepper, divided

4 ½ lb small pork spareribs (side or back)

1 Tbsp extra virgin olive oil or pure coconut oil

4–5 cloves garlic, finely chopped

¼ cup peeled and finely chopped fresh ginger

1 ½ cups packed brown sugar

1 ½ cups filtered water

5 Tbsp soy sauce

1 ½ Tbsp dry mustard

1. Fill a large pot with water and bring to a boil. Add the onion, bay leaf, salt, and ½ tsp pepper.

2. Cut the ribs into sections just small enough to fit in the pot. Add the ribs to the boiling water and cook for 2 to 3 minutes. Cover, reduce the heat, and simmer for 20 minutes or until the meat is tender.

3. While the ribs are simmering, prepare the sauce. Heat the oil in a heavy pot large enough to fit the ribs. Add the garlic and ginger and sauté on medium heat for 4 to 5 minutes. Set aside.

4. In a medium bowl, mix the brown sugar, water, soy sauce, dry mustard, and the remaining ½ tsp pepper. Whisk to dissolve the mustard.

5. Add the sugar and mustard mixture to the ginger and garlic. Stir, then set aside.

6. Remove the spareribs from the water. Slice the meat between the bones to make individual ribs.

7. Bring the sauce ingredients to a boil. Add the spareribs to the sauce, return to a boil, and simmer for 20 to 25 minutes, basting occasionally. Alternatively, transfer all ingredients to a slow cooker and cook on low for 3 hours, stirring the ribs occasionally to coat with sauce.

8. When cooked, transfer the ribs and sauce to a baking dish. Bake at 400°F for 8 to 10 minutes, basting the ribs with sauce several times.

9. Remove the ribs and place on a serving platter.

10. Transfer the sauce to a medium pan. Bring the sauce to a boil and reduce to thicken. Pour over the ribs and serve.

→ TIP Serve these ribs with Oven-Roasted Herb Potatoes (see page 33) and Cabbage Salad (see page 16).

Chicken Kiev

SERVES 4

Elegant, tasty, and very simple to make, this dish can be prepared ahead and refrigerated until it's time to bake it. When I was a young farmwife, this recipe was the very first "fancy entrée" I prepared as a special dinner for guests. I didn't own a meat mallet at the time, so when I came to the part of the recipe that said to flatten the chicken breast, I used Bill's hammer covered with waxed paper—it definitely worked!

4 whole chicken breasts, skinned, deboned, and split into halves

½ cup fine dry bread crumbs

½ cup grated Parmesan cheese

1 ½ tsp dried oregano, divided

½ tsp garlic salt

¼ tsp freshly ground black pepper

¼ cup unsalted butter, softened

1 Tbsp chopped fresh parsley, plus additional leaves for garnish

¼ lb Monterey Jack cheese, cut into 8 strips, ½ inch thick and 1 ½ inches long

5 Tbsp melted butter or melted pure coconut oil

1. Preheat the oven to 425°F.

2. Place each chicken breast between sheets of parchment paper, one at a time. With the flat side of a mallet, gently pound the breasts until each is about ¼ inch thick. Set aside.

3. In a rimmed pan, combine bread crumbs, Parmesan, 1 tsp oregano, garlic salt, and pepper.

4. In a small bowl, stir together the softened butter, parsley, and remaining oregano. Add more garlic salt here if you like.

5. Spread about ½ Tbsp of the herb butter mixture on each breast.

6. Top each breast with one slice of cheese.

7. Roll the breast from the wide end toward the narrow end, making sure to pinch the sides and tuck in as you go.

8. Dip each rolled breast in the melted butter, then in the bread crumbs, coating all sides.

9. Arrange the breasts, loose side down, in a 9- × 13-inch baking dish. If necessary, use a wooden pick to hold each rolled chicken breast together, and remove the picks before serving.

10. Bake in the preheated oven for 20 to 25 minutes.

Roast Chicken and Gravy

SERVES 4-6

This has been the traditional Sunday dinner at our family table for years. The gravy is light and goes perfectly with mashed, riced, or whipped potatoes.

. . . .

6 lb fresh whole roasting chicken

1 tsp extra virgin olive oil or butter

½ cup chicken stock or water from cooking potatoes (for the gravy)

2 tsp unbleached all-purpose flour

1 cup cold filtered water

Sea salt and freshly ground black pepper to taste

1. Preheat the oven to 375°F.

2. Remove the chicken giblets and discard or keep for other uses. Discard any fat and remove any quills with tweezers. Rinse the chicken skin and cavity with cold tap water. Wipe the cavity with a paper towel soaked in vinegar.

3. Rub the skin of the chicken with olive oil or butter. Tie the legs together using kitchen twine. Place the chicken in a medium roasting pan, breast side up, tucking the wing tips underneath the bird. Set on the middle rack of the preheated oven.

4. Roast, uncovered, for 2 hours or until a meat thermometer inserted in the meatiest part of the chicken reads 180°F. Baste the chicken with pan drippings as it roasts.

5. Remove the chicken from the pan and place on a serving dish, keeping it warm in a tent of aluminum foil and a towel.

6. Skim and discard the fat from the pan drippings (see Tip). Scrape the bits of meat from the pan and transfer all to a heavy pot.

7. Bring to a boil over medium heat and stir until the liquid is reduced by a third.

8. Add the stock or potato water and bring back to a gentle boil. Reduce the heat and simmer, stirring, for 5 to 10 minutes.

9. In a small container with a tight-fitting lid or in a gravy shaker, add the flour to the cold water. Shake vigorously until no lumps remain.

10. Increase the pan heat to medium-high and whisk in the flour and water mixture. Bring to a boil, then simmer for 5 minutes or until thickened, whisking often. Add salt and pepper to taste.

→ **TIP** A quick way to remove fat from drippings is to place the drippings in a medium bowl in the freezer for 5 to 7 minutes. The fat will rise to the top when cooled. Skim the fat with a large spoon and discard.

To thicken gravy, add more flour; for thinner gravy, increase the amount of stock or water.

Fish and Chips

SERVES 4

Halibut is my personal choice for fish and chips, but any dense, white fish like cod or flounder can be substituted in this recipe. Serve whichever fish you choose with the French-Fried Potatoes (see next page). Cook the potatoes first and keep them warm in the oven until your fish is ready.

. . . .

1 ½ lb halibut or cod fillet

1 Tbsp fresh lemon juice

1 ½ cups unbleached all-purpose flour, divided

1 tsp sea salt

1 tsp freshly ground black pepper

½ tsp paprika

1 cup beer

3 cups pure peanut oil

Malt or white vinegar

Lemon wedges

Tartar sauce

1. Preheat the oven to 300°F.

2. Cut the fish into medium-size serving pieces and sprinkle with the lemon juice.

3. In a medium bowl, combine 1 cup of the flour with the salt, pepper, paprika, and beer.

4. Dredge the fish in the remaining ½ cup flour, then in the beer batter.

5. In a heavy pot, heat the oil to 375°F, or use an electric deep-fryer on the fish setting. (If you made french fries beforehand, add 1 cup of oil for a total of 3 cups.) Cook the fish for 4 to 6 minutes or until the batter is crispy and golden. Repeat until all the fish has been cooked.

6. Drain the fish on paper towels, then transfer to a baking dish and keep warm in the preheated oven.

7. Serve the fish and chips on a platter with vinegar, lemon wedges, and tartar sauce.

→ TIP Fish and chips are made even better with Cabbage Salad (see page 16).

Continued overleaf…

FRENCH-FRIED POTATOES

In Quebec and other parts of Canada, "chip wagons" are common on the roadside where freshly peeled potatoes become *patates frites*, or french fries. I always leave the skins on when I make them. Using peanut oil to fry potatoes really lets the potato taste come through!

SERVES 3–4

4–6 medium baking potatoes
(like russets), scrubbed
2 cups pure peanut oil
Sea salt to taste

1. Wash and dry the potatoes. Using a slicer or sharp knife, cut the potatoes into french-fry lengths. Spread the cut potatoes on a tea towel.

2. In a very heavy saucepan or pot, heat the oil to 375°F. Cook the potatoes in small batches until golden brown. Cooking time will vary depending on the size of the fries. For the size pictured in the photo, this will take 5 to 8 minutes. Transfer each batch to a plate lined with a paper towel to absorb extra oil. Salt if desired.

→ TIP To cook french fries for a group, partly cook the potatoes for half the total frying time (usually 3 to 4 minutes) and then drain on a paper towel. When ready to serve, fry them again in oil at 375°F until golden brown. Drain and salt.

Cooking temperature is critical. Cooking at a very low temperature will make the potatoes absorb and retain oil and become soggy. Cooking at a very high temperature will cook the outside of the potato too quickly and leave the inside uncooked.

If you use an electric deep-fryer, select the french-fry setting and follow the manufacturer's instructions.

Shrimp Tacos

SERVES 2-4

Shrimp tacos can be the main meal or served as a snack.

1 Tbsp pure coconut oil

1 lb cooked and peeled medium shrimp

6 small soft flour tortillas

1 cup Salsa (see page 6)

½ cup tartar sauce

1 small onion, chopped

¼ cabbage, finely shredded

3 Tbsp fresh lemon juice

Handful of fresh cilantro, chopped

12 lemon wedges

1. In a heavy skillet, heat the oil on medium-high. Add the cooked shrimp and stir until warmed through.

2. On a flat skillet or griddle, heat the tortillas for 30 to 45 seconds on each side. Transfer to a serving platter and cover to keep warm.

3. Fill each taco with shrimp, salsa, and tartar sauce to taste. Top with onions and shredded cabbage and sprinkle with lemon juice. Garnish with cilantro and serve with lemon wedges.

Chocolate-Covered Potato Chips 76

Potato Chip Chocolate Squares 78

Apple Crisp 79

Nanaimo Bars 81

Chocolate Chip and Nut Cookies 82

Granddad's Cookies 84

Shortbread Cookies 85

Oatmeal Raisin Cookies 86

Grandma Kerr's Brownies 87

Carrot Cake 89

Flourless Chocolate Cake 90

One-Bowl Birthday Cake 92

Tea Biscuits 93

Cranberry Orange Scones 94

Vickie's Baked Granola 97

Zucchini Loaf 98

Banana Muffins 101

Bran Muffins 102

Best Pie Crust 104

Apple Pie 106

Lemon Meringue Pie 108

Pumpkin Pie 109

Lemon Curd Tarts 111

Raspberry Tarts 112

Desserts AND BAKING

Chocolate-Covered Potato Chips

YIELD: SERVES 2

You can make your own potato chips (see page 31) for this recipe or use them from the bag. Select large chips that are not curled. The flatter the chip, the more you can cover it with chocolate.

· ·

Two 1 oz squares semi-sweet baking chocolate
12 large potato chips with sea salt or no salt

1. Melt the chocolate in the microwave or on the stovetop in a glass or metal bowl over a pot of boiling water.

2. Hold the edge of a chip over the melted chocolate, and use a spoon to spread the chocolate on one side of the chip. Repeat for all chips.

3. Arrange the chocolate-covered chips, chocolate side up, on parchment or waxed paper. Chill for 10 minutes and serve.

Potato Chip Chocolate Squares

YIELD: 12 SQUARES

Bill and I concocted this salty and sweet treat one Friday night because we loved eating a Jersey Milk chocolate bar mixed with potato chips.

½ cup unsalted butter

¼ cup granulated sugar

6 Tbsp unsweetened cocoa powder (like Fry's)

1 egg, beaten

1 ½ cups crushed potato chips with salt

1 cup finely shredded unsweetened coconut

1. Melt the butter, sugar, and cocoa in a very heavy saucepan on low heat.

2. Add the beaten egg, stirring to cook and thicken. Remove from the heat.

3. Stir in the crushed potato chips and coconut.

4. Pat into a greased 8- × 8-inch pan and press down with your fingers to spread evenly.

5. Refrigerate for 30 minutes, then cut into squares.

→ TIP Use a rolling pin to crush the potato chips.

Apple Crisp

This recipe has two layers. The apple mixture covers the pan bottom, and the oatmeal layer makes the topping.

. . . .

5–6 large baking apples, peeled and sliced

¼ cup filtered water

½ cup plus 1 Tbsp packed brown sugar, divided

1 Tbsp fresh lemon juice

½ tsp ground nutmeg

¼ tsp ground cinnamon

⅓ cup unbleached all-purpose flour

½ cup rolled oats

½ tsp sea salt

5 Tbsp unsalted butter, chilled

6 pecans, halved

1. Preheat the oven to 375°F.

2. Arrange the sliced apples in the bottom of a greased 8- × 8-inch baking dish.

3. In a small bowl, mix the water, 1 Tbsp brown sugar, lemon juice, nutmeg, and cinnamon. Sprinkle this mixture evenly over the sliced apples.

4. In a medium bowl, mix the flour, oats, remaining ½ cup brown sugar, and salt.

5. Cut the butter into the oat mixture with a pastry cutter or two knives until the butter is in very small pieces.

6. Spread the oat mixture over the sliced apples. Arrange the pecans on top.

7. Bake for 30 minutes until the edges bubble. Increase the oven temperature to 425°F and bake for 5 more minutes to crisp the crumb topping.

8. Cool at least 2 hours before serving.

→ TIP Use only a variety of cooking apples that will soften during baking, like McIntosh.

Nanaimo Bars

YIELD: 24 SMALL SQUARES

Nanaimo Bars are a uniquely Canadian dessert that take their name from Nanaimo, British Columbia. Make this no-bake, three-layer recipe in easy-to-follow steps.

1 cup plus 2 Tbsp unsalted butter, divided

¼ cup granulated sugar

5 Tbsp unsweetened cocoa powder (like Fry's)

1 egg, beaten

1 ½ cups graham wafer crumbs

1 cup finely shredded unsweetened coconut

2 Tbsp heavy cream

2 ½ Tbsp vanilla custard powder
   (1 envelope, like Bird's)

2 cups icing (confectioner's) sugar

½ tsp pure vanilla extract

Three 1 oz squares semi-sweet baking chocolate

1. Melt ½ cup butter, the granulated sugar, and the cocoa in a very heavy saucepan on low heat.

2. Whisk in the beaten egg. Cook, stirring constantly to thicken.

3. Remove from the heat. Stir in the graham crumbs and coconut.

4. Turn the chocolate mixture into an ungreased 8- × 8-inch pan. Press down with your fingers to spread evenly.

5. Cream the ½ cup butter, cream, custard powder, icing sugar, and vanilla together. Beat well with a spoon. Spread over the crumb layer.

6. Melt the chocolate and the remaining 2 Tbsp butter in a heavy saucepan on very low heat.

7. Drizzle the melted chocolate over the second layer, spreading evenly with a back of a spoon. Refrigerate for at least 2 hours.

8. Bring to room temperature and cut into squares.

Chocolate Chip and Nut Cookies

YIELD: 24 COOKIES

These are so good any time! Use an ungreased baking sheet to make soft, chewy cookies. For crispy cookies, line the baking sheet with parchment paper.

. . . .

1 cup unsalted butter, softened
¾ cup granulated sugar
¾ cup packed brown sugar
2 eggs, beaten
2 ¼ cups unbleached all-purpose flour

1 tsp baking soda
½ tsp sea salt
1 cup chopped pecans
2 cups (one 12 oz bag) semi-sweet
   chocolate chips

1. Preheat the oven to 375°F.

2. In a large mixing bowl, cream the butter. Stir in the sugars and mix with a wooden spoon until creamy.

3. Fold the eggs into the creamed mixture.

4. In a separate bowl, mix the flour, baking soda, and salt. Add the flour mixture to the creamed butter, mixing lightly. Do not overmix or the cookies will be tough. Gently fold in the pecans and chocolate chips.

5. Cover and chill the dough for at least 20 minutes. (Refrigerate overnight if you want fresh cookies the next day.)

6. Drop the dough by rounded spoonfuls on a baking sheet about 2 inches apart (see Tip).

7. Bake for 8 to 10 minutes or until very lightly browned (the centre will still be soft).

8. Cool on the baking sheet for 1 minute, then transfer to a wire rack to cool completely. Fresh-baked cookies taste best, but you can also store these in an airtight container for 3 to 4 days.

→   TIP A hot baking sheet will melt cookie dough before it bakes. Cool the cookie sheet between batches for best results.

Refrigerate unused dough in an airtight container for up to a week. You can also freeze unbaked dough for up to 2 weeks and thaw before baking.

Granddad's Cookies

These cookies are made with coconut and oatmeal and were Grandpa Kerr's favourite.

· ·

1 cup unsalted butter, softened
   (or ½ cup butter and ½ cup shortening)
2 cups packed brown sugar
2 eggs, beaten

2 cups unbleached all-purpose flour
½ tsp baking soda
2 cups organic rolled oats
1 cup finely shredded unsweetened coconut

1. Preheat the oven to 400°F.

2. In a large bowl, blend the butter and brown sugar. Add the eggs and mix well.

3. In a separate bowl, mix the flour, baking soda, oats, and coconut.

4. Add the dry ingredients to the butter mixture. Blend with a wooden spoon. Do not overmix or the cookies will be tough. Refrigerate the dough for 20 minutes.

5. With floured hands, take about 2 Tbsp of dough and roll it into smooth balls.

6. Space about 2 inches apart on a greased baking sheet. Use a fork to partially flatten the balls and to make a design.

7. Bake for 8 to 12 minutes, until just lightly browned around the edges.

8. Remove from the oven and leave on the baking sheet for about 1 minute. Carefully transfer the cookies to a wire rack to cool completely. Store in an airtight container for up to 1 week.

Shortbread Cookies

YIELD: 24 COOKIES

These are signature cookies in the Kerr households around the holidays. Grandma always made them with a tiny piece of maraschino cherry on top, so I do, too.

. . . .

1 lb unsalted butter, softened
1 cup icing (confectioner's) sugar
½ cup cornstarch
3 cups unbleached all-purpose flour

1. Preheat the oven to 350°F.

2. In a large bowl, cream the butter, icing sugar, and cornstarch.

3. Add the flour gradually, beating after each addition. Beat until the mixture is light and looks like whipped cream.

4. Chill for 20 minutes.

5. Roll out the dough on a floured board until it is ½ inch thick. Cut small, round shapes with a cookie cutter or the rim of a small drinking glass.

6. Arrange the cut cookies on an ungreased baking sheet.

7. Bake on the middle rack of the oven for 15 minutes or until golden around the edges. Do not overbake.

8. Cool on the baking sheet for 1 minute, and then remove the cookies to a wire rack to cool completely.

9. Serve immediately or store in an airtight container for up to 4 days. Freeze for up to 2 months.

→ TIP For thicker cookies, roll the dough into small balls by hand and arrange on an ungreased baking sheet. Flatten with a fork.

You can decorate the cookies with a sliver of candied maraschino cherry or a pecan gently pushed into the centre of each cookie before baking, or sprinkle coloured candy on the cut cookies and press into the dough very gently before baking.

Oatmeal Raisin Cookies

YIELD: 24 COOKIES

After a day at school, the children would return home to the farm and often be greeted with a plate of these cookies and a glass of milk.

½ cup plus 6 Tbsp unsalted butter, softened

¾ cup packed brown sugar

½ cup granulated sugar

2 eggs, beaten

1 tsp pure vanilla extract

3 cups organic rolled oats

1 ½ cups unbleached all-purpose flour

¼ cup wheat germ

1 tsp ground cinnamon

1 tsp baking soda

½ tsp sea salt

1 cup raisins

1. Preheat the oven to 350°F.

2. In a large bowl, beat the butter and the sugars with a wooden spoon until light and fluffy.

3. Add the eggs and vanilla and beat until smooth.

4. In a separate bowl, combine the oats, flour, wheat germ, cinnamon, baking soda, and salt, and mix well.

5. Add the oat mixture to the creamed butter and stir gently. Add the raisins.

6. Cover and refrigerate the dough for 30 minutes before baking.

7. Drop the dough by rounded spoonfuls about 2 inches apart onto an ungreased baking sheet.

8. Bake for 8 to 10 minutes or until golden brown around the edges.

9. Cool on the baking sheet for 1 minute, then transfer to a wire rack to cool completely. Store in an airtight container for up to 1 week or freeze for up to 1 month.

→ TIP Add lecithin, oat bran, protein powder, or additional nutritious ingredients to these cookies. The kids will never notice.

Grandma Kerr's Brownies

YIELD: 12–16 BROWNIES

This family favourite is easy to prepare and delicious. The secret to making chewy, chocolate-rich brownies is to watch them carefully and not overbake.

. . . .

BROWNIES

½ cup unsalted butter, softened

1 cup granulated sugar

½ cup unsweetened cocoa powder (like Fry's)

¼–½ cup boiling water

2 large eggs, well beaten

½ cup unbleached all-purpose flour

1 tsp pure vanilla extract

½ cup chopped walnuts (optional)

FROSTING

2 Tbsp unsalted butter, softened

½ cup icing (confectioner's) sugar

¼ tsp pure vanilla extract

2 heaping Tbsp unsweetened cocoa powder (like Fry's)

About 2 Tbsp boiling water

1. Preheat the oven to 350°F if you are using a metal pan, or 325°F for glass.

2. Lightly grease an 8- × 8-inch pan and sprinkle it with flour to prevent the brownies from sticking to the pan while baking.

3. In a medium mixing bowl, cream the butter until light and fluffy. Add the sugar and mix well.

4. In a small bowl, blend the cocoa with just enough hot water to make a thick paste. Add the cocoa paste to the creamed butter mixture and blend.

5. Add the beaten eggs to the cocoa mixture and beat well. Gradually add the flour, stirring until smooth. Stir in the vanilla. Fold in the nuts, if desired.

6. Spread the batter in the pan all the way to each edge, and place on the middle rack of the preheated oven. After the brownies have baked for 20 minutes, insert a wooden pick in the centre. If it comes out clean, remove the pan from the oven. If not, check for doneness again in a few minutes. Very tiny bubbles will form across the top when it is baked completely.

7. Cool the brownies in the pan for at least 2 hours before frosting.

8. To make the frosting, in a medium bowl, cream the butter. Sift in the icing sugar and blend well. Add the vanilla and blend well.

9. In a separate bowl, blend the cocoa with just enough hot water to make a smooth paste. Add the cocoa to the icing sugar mixture and beat. If the frosting is too thick to spread, add a few drops of milk.

10. Use a wet knife to spread the frosting on the cooled brownies. Store at room temperature covered with aluminum foil to preserve freshness.

Carrot Cake

You'll need one large bowl for the liquid ingredients and another for the dry ingredients. My niece partly credits her marriage proposal to her baking "Auntie Vickie's Carrot Cake" for her future husband.

....

CAKE

4 eggs

1 ½ cups pure coconut oil or peanut oil

2 cups granulated sugar

1 tsp pure vanilla extract

3 heaping cups grated carrots

2 cups unbleached all-purpose flour

2 tsp baking soda

2 tsp baking powder

1 tsp ground cinnamon

1 tsp sea salt

½ cup chopped walnuts

½ cup raisins

FROSTING

½ cup unsalted butter, softened

4 oz cream cheese, softened

2 cups icing (confectioner's) sugar, sifted

1 tsp pure vanilla extract

¼ cup chopped walnuts

1. Preheat the oven to 375°F if you are using a metal pan, or 350°F for glass.

2. Lightly oil and flour a 13- × 9-inch glass or metal baking pan. Line the bottom of the pan with parchment paper or lightly oil the pan to make it easy to remove the cake after baking.

3. In a large mixing bowl, beat the eggs well on medium speed. Add the oil, sugar, and vanilla and beat until well blended. Fold in the grated carrots and blend well.

4. In a second large mixing bowl, sift together all the dry ingredients (flour through salt).

5. Add the wet ingredients to the dry and mix until combined.

6. Add the walnuts and the raisins. Pour the batter into the pan.

7. Bake on the middle rack of the oven for 45 to 50 minutes. Check for doneness after 45 minutes by inserting a wooden pick into the centre of the cake. If the pick comes out clean, the cake is done. If not, allow the cake to bake for 5 to 7 minutes longer, then check again. Repeat as necessary. The sides and top of the cake should be golden brown when done. Cool the cake in the pan before frosting.

8. To make the frosting, in a medium bowl, cream the butter, then add the cream cheese and blend together until there are no lumps. Gradually add the sifted icing sugar, blending well after each addition.

9. Add the vanilla and mix. Fold in the walnuts.

10. Frost the cake after it has cooled completely. Cut into squares and serve, or cover and refrigerate, then cut into squares and serve.

Flourless Chocolate Cake

SERVES 12–14

This cake is a family favourite, and it's absolutely decadent when covered and stored in the refrigerator for two or three days before serving. You'll need two pans that fit one inside the other for this recipe.

½ cup filtered water

¼ tsp sea salt

¾ cup granulated sugar

Eighteen 1 oz squares semi-sweet baking chocolate

1 cup unsalted butter, softened

6 eggs

1. Preheat the oven to 300°F. Grease a 10-inch round cake pan. Line with parchment paper and set aside.

2. In a small saucepan over medium heat, combine the water, salt, and sugar. Stir until the salt and sugar are completely dissolved, then set aside.

3. Melt the chocolate in a large bowl over a pot of boiling water or in a microwave oven.

4. Cut the butter into 10 to 12 pieces and beat into the chocolate, one piece at a time.

5. Add the hot sugar water and beat.

6. Slowly beat in the eggs, one at a time, until blended.

7. Pour the batter into the prepared pan. Set that cake pan in a larger pan that has been filled with very hot water about halfway up the sides of the cake pan.

8. Bake the cake in the water bath for 45 to 50 minutes. Use a wooden pick to test for doneness. The centre will be cooked if the pick is dry, though the cake may still look wet.

9. Remove the cake pan from the hot water bath. Cool to room temperature, wrap tightly with plastic wrap, and chill overnight or for several days in the fridge. To unmould, dip the bottom of the cake pan in hot water for 10 seconds and invert onto a serving plate.

One-Bowl Birthday Cake

YIELD: 12–16 SLICES OF CAKE OR 12–16 CUPCAKES

All you need to prepare this birthday cake is a single large mixing bowl!

. . . .

CAKE

2 large eggs

1 cup pure coconut oil

1 cup buttermilk (or curdle whole milk with 1 Tbsp vinegar)

1 tsp pure vanilla extract

1 ½ cups granulated sugar

½ cup packed brown sugar

2 cups unbleached all-purpose flour

1 Tbsp baking soda

¼ tsp sea salt

¾ cup unsweetened cocoa powder (like Fry's)

1 cup boiling water

FROSTING

¼ cup unsalted butter, softened

2 cups icing (confectioner's) sugar, sifted

½ tsp pure vanilla extract

6 Tbsp milk

1. Preheat the oven to 325°F. Line two or three 8- or 9-inch round baking pans with parchment paper, or a 12-cup muffin tin with paper liners.

2. In a large mixing bowl, beat the eggs until frothy. Add the oil and continue to beat.

3. Add the buttermilk and vanilla and beat. Gradually add the sugars, beating after each addition.

4. Gradually add the flour, baking soda, and salt to the egg mixture, beating after each addition.

5. Blend half of the cocoa into the batter. Carefully add the hot water to the batter and beat on low speed. Add the remaining cocoa and beat until smooth.

6. Divide the batter equally between the prepared pans or muffin tins.

7. Bake in the preheated oven for 50 minutes. Check for doneness by inserting a wooden pick into the centre of each cake. If the pick comes out clean, the cakes are done. If not, allow the cakes to bake for a few minutes longer, then check again. Repeat as necessary. When cool enough to handle (about 15 minutes), turn the cakes out onto a wire rack to cool completely.

8. To make the frosting, cream the butter and half of the icing sugar together until there are no lumps. Add the vanilla and half of the milk and mix to a smooth consistency.

9. Add the remaining icing sugar and milk. Beat until smooth. For a thicker consistency, add more icing sugar. To thin the icing, add more milk.

10. With a wet knife, spread the frosting between the layers and on the sides and top of the cooled cake.

→ **TIP** To keep brown sugar soft during storage, place a quarter slice of bread into the sugar container and seal tightly. Replace the bread occasionally and you'll always have soft brown sugar.

Tea Biscuits

YIELD: EIGHT TO TEN 3-INCH TEA BISCUITS

Out on the farm, Grandma could whip up a batch of tea biscuits at the drop of a hat! The ingredients are simple and were always at hand, with no wait time required for proofing or kneading. Warm tea biscuits with jam and cheese would appear at tea breaks or served for lunch or supper as a quick, warm, tasty bread substitute to farmhands and unexpected guests alike.

. . . .

2 cups unbleached all-purpose flour

1 Tbsp baking powder

¼ tsp baking soda

½ cup shortening, chilled

¾ cup half-and-half cream or whole milk

1 tsp white vinegar

1. Preheat the oven to 425°F.

2. Combine all dry ingredients well.

3. Add the shortening and use a pastry cutter or two knives to cut it into the flour to make small crumbs.

4. In a medium bowl, combine the cream or milk and vinegar to produce curdled milk.

5. Add only enough curdled milk to the flour to moisten it and allow the dough to stick together. Don't handle the dough too much.

6. On a well-floured surface, gently roll out the dough to 1½ inches thick.

7. Cut rounds in the dough with a biscuit cutter. Space the rounds apart on a greased baking sheet. Prick the top of each biscuit with a fork to allow steam to escape while baking.

8. Bake for 15 to 18 minutes or until golden brown.

9. Serve warm or store leftover tea biscuits in an airtight container for up to 3 days.

Cranberry Orange Scones

YIELD: 16 SCONES

I sometimes substitute chocolate chips, raisins, or currants for the cranberries.

Basic Scone Mix (see recipe below)

⅓ cup granulated sugar, plus more for sprinkling

2 cups plus 1 Tbsp cold heavy cream, divided

½ cup chopped walnuts

¾ cup dried cranberries, chopped

1 Tbsp orange zest

1. Preheat the oven to 425°F.

2. In a large mixing bowl, combine the basic scone mix and sugar. Stir in 2 cups cream. Mix gently.

3. Fold in the walnuts, cranberries, and orange zest.

4. Stir until a dough begins to form. The dough will still be a bit sticky.

5. Turn the dough onto a floured surface and knead about 10 times until the dough sticks together.

6. With well-floured hands, divide the dough in half and pat out to make two circles 1 inch thick.

7. Cut each circle into 8 wedges and place on an ungreased baking sheet.

8. Brush each wedge with the remaining 1 Tbsp cream. Sprinkle with sugar, if desired.

9. Bake for 15 to 18 minutes until lightly browned.

BASIC SCONE MIX

Use this scone mix to make Cranberry Orange Scones or any scones you can imagine.

YIELD: 16 SCONES

6 cups unbleached all-purpose flour

3 Tbsp baking powder

1 ½ tsp sea salt

1 cup plus 3 Tbsp unsalted butter, cold

1. Place the flour, baking powder, and salt in a large bowl. Use a pastry cutter or two knives to cut the butter into the flour mixture to make small crumbs.

2. Refrigerate for use in any scone recipe.

Vickie's Baked Granola

SERVES 20

Use organic rolled oats and add your favourite nuts! This is great for a quick and nutritious breakfast; just add milk.

. . . .

4 cups organic rolled oats

1 cup finely shredded unsweetened coconut

1 cup chopped walnuts or pecans

1 cup chopped cashews

½ cup sunflower seeds

½ cup flaxseeds

½ cup packed brown sugar

1–2 tsp ground cinnamon (adjust to your taste)

1 tsp sea salt (optional)

½ cup pure coconut oil

½ cup filtered water

1 Tbsp honey

1 tsp pure vanilla extract

1 cup raisins

1 cup dried cranberries

1. Preheat the oven to 300°F.

2. Grease a large jelly-roll pan (a rimmed baking sheet).

3. In a large mixing bowl, combine all dry ingredients except the raisins and cranberries.

4. In a medium mixing bowl, combine the oil, water, and honey (warmed first to make it easier to blend with the water).

5. Gradually add the liquid ingredients to the dry ingredients and mix until the oats are well coated.

6. Evenly spread the mixture onto the pan and bake for 45 minutes or until golden.

7. Use a spatula to turn the granola every 10 to 15 minutes to allow for even baking.

8. Cool completely, then add the raisins and cranberries. Store the granola in an airtight container for up to 4 weeks.

Zucchini Loaf

YIELD: 2 MEDIUM OR 3 MINI LOAVES

When you have a great harvest of zucchini from your garden and don't know what to do with it all, try making this simple and delicious loaf. I make small ones and freeze them to give as gifts. My son tells me the aroma of baking zucchini loaf always reminds him of home.

....

3 eggs

1 ½ cups granulated sugar

1 cup pure coconut oil or extra virgin olive oil

2 tsp pure vanilla extract

2 heaping cups unpeeled, seeded, and shredded zucchini

3 cups unbleached all-purpose flour

1 tsp baking powder

1 tsp baking soda

1 tsp sea salt

1 Tbsp ground cinnamon

½ Tbsp ground nutmeg

½ cup chopped walnuts

½ cup raisins

1. Preheat the oven to 350°F. Grease and flour two 9- × 5-inch or four mini 5½- × 3½ × 1½-inch loaf pans.

2. In a large bowl, beat the eggs well on medium speed. Add the sugar, oil, and vanilla and beat.

3. Stir in the shredded zucchini and coat well.

4. In a separate bowl, combine the flour, baking powder, baking soda, salt, cinnamon, and nutmeg.

5. Slowly mix in the dry ingredients to the zucchini mixture. Carefully fold in the walnuts and raisins.

6. Pour the batter into the prepared loaf pans.

7. Bake for 45 to 55 minutes or until the top and sides are golden brown. Check for doneness by inserting a wooden pick in the centre of each loaf. When the pick comes out clean, remove the loaves from the oven. Cool before wrapping or freezing.

Banana Muffins

YIELD: 12–16 MUFFINS

This recipe is a great way to use very ripe bananas. Is there anything better than waking up to warm, delicious muffins in the morning?

. . . .

½ cup unsalted butter, softened

1 cup granulated sugar

3 eggs

1 tsp baking soda

2 tsp baking powder

½ tsp sea salt

½ tsp pure vanilla extract

¼ cup sour milk or buttermilk (see Tip)

3 medium-size very ripe bananas

2 cups unbleached all-purpose flour

1. Preheat the oven to 375°F.

2. In a medium bowl and with a wooden spoon, cream together the butter and sugar until smooth.

3. In a separate bowl, beat the eggs on medium speed until frothy.

4. Add the eggs to the sugar and butter mixture and beat until light and fluffy. Set aside.

5. In a small bowl, mix the baking soda, baking powder, salt, vanilla, and sour milk. Set aside.

6. In a large bowl, mash the bananas. Add the sour milk mixture to the bananas and stir well to combine.

7. Alternately add the flour and the butter mixture to the banana mixture, mixing gently after each addition. Do not overmix.

8. Fill greased muffin tins with the batter to about three-quarters full.

9. Bake for 20 to 25 minutes or until the muffin tops are golden.

10. Cool the muffins in the tins for 3 minutes, then transfer to a wire rack to cool completely.

→   TIP If you don't have sour milk or buttermilk handy, mix ¼ cup whole milk with 1 tsp vinegar to curdle the milk.

Bran Muffins

YIELD: 12–16 MUFFINS

These moist muffins are filled with wheat bran, flaxseeds, and wheat germ. Wheat bran is the outer layer of the grain and rich in fibre and nutrients, and what bran cereal is made of. Wheat germ contains naturally occurring polyunsaturated fat.

. . . .

2 eggs

1 cup pure coconut oil or extra virgin olive oil

1 cup packed brown sugar

2 cups bran cereal morsels (like All-Bran)

2 cups whole milk

2 cups unbleached all-purpose flour

1 Tbsp wheat germ

1 Tbsp ground flaxseeds

2 tsp baking soda

2 tsp baking powder

1 tsp sea salt

1 cup prepared mincemeat (see Tip)

1. Preheat the oven to 350°F.

2. In a large bowl, beat the eggs. Add the oil and brown sugar and beat well.

3. In a separate large bowl, combine the cereal morsels and milk and set aside until the milk is absorbed, about 5 minutes.

4. In a third large bowl, combine the flour, wheat germ, flaxseeds, baking soda, baking powder, and salt.

5. Add the flour and milk mixtures alternately to the oil and egg mixture, mixing gently with each addition.

6. Add the mincemeat, blending well with a wooden spoon.

7. Fill greased muffin tins to about three-quarters full.

8. Bake on the middle rack of the oven for 20 to 25 minutes. The edges of the muffins should pull slightly away from the sides of the tin.

9. Remove from the oven and cool the muffins in the tins for 5 minutes before transferring them to a wire rack. Cool completely and store in an airtight container.

→   TIP Mincemeat contains raisins and can be purchased at most markets and grocery stores in the baking section.

Best Pie Crust

YIELD: 1 DOUBLE-CRUST PIE

This is the perfect pie crust recipe that changed my life.

· ·

2¾ cups unbleached all-purpose flour,
    plus more for dusting

¾ tsp sea salt

¾ tsp brown sugar

1 cup chilled pure lard, or ½ cup chilled vegetable
    shortening and ½ cup pure lard, cut in 12–14 pieces

3 Tbsp ice-cold filtered water

1 egg

1 Tbsp white vinegar

1. In a large mixing bowl, combine the flour, salt, and brown sugar.

2. Add the lard, cutting it in with a pastry cutter or two butter knives in a criss-cross manner to make pea-size pieces.

3. In a separate bowl, combine the cold water, egg, and vinegar and stir.

4. Add just enough of the cold liquid into the flour mixture to moisten the pastry so it clings together when stirred.

5. Use your hands to gather the pastry and divide it into 2 balls to be rolled out later. Cover and chill the pastry in the refrigerator for 20 minutes.

6. Place a large square of waxed or parchment paper on the counter and dust lightly with flour.

7. Place 1 ball of dough in the centre, push it down to flatten, dust with flour, and place another square of paper on top. Push down with the palm of your hand to spread the dough into a flat disc. Remove the top paper.

8. Flour a rolling pin. Roll the dough evenly into a circle to fit the pie plate, with enough extra dough to hang over the edge. While rolling the dough, sprinkle it with flour so it won't stick to the rolling pin.

9. Invert the circle of pastry over the pie plate, gently easing it into place, then remove the paper. Carefully adjust and centre the pastry in the pie plate.

10. Follow the filling, shaping, and baking instructions of your recipe. For double-crust pies, check the pie often to confirm that the top crust isn't baking too fast and burning as temperatures may vary from oven to oven. When baking fruit pies, cover the bottom of your oven with aluminum foil, or slide a baking sheet under the baking pie to catch spills and make cleanup easier.

→ **TIP** This recipe will make enough for one double-crust pie or two single-crust pies. If you're making a single-crust pie, wrap the second ball of dough tightly and store in the fridge or freezer until you want to make another pie.

If the recipe calls for a blind-baked pie crust, prick the bottom of the unbaked pie shell with a fork to allow steam to escape and prevent bubbles from forming while baking, or line the pastry with aluminum foil and rice or pie weights. Bake at 400°F for 5 minutes, then reduce the oven to 300°F and bake for 10 more minutes or until golden brown.

THE PIE THAT CHANGED MY LIFE

As a city girl who hadn't taken much interest in baking or cooking before becoming a farmer's wife, I quickly learned something new and humbling: on the farm, a woman's worth was measured by her ability to accomplish several vital tasks, and one of them was baking the perfect pie.

I tried hard to make a good pie. I attempted to follow instructions from Bill's mother about how to mix, chill, and roll out the dough and then actually get it into the waiting pie plate. And I threw away lots of pie dough in failed attempts to create that perfect pie crust. On those days, Bill would only smile when he walked by the trash can and saw uncooked pastry and a kitchen covered in flour.

It was a very early morning in mid-July; the air was hot and humid, and the kitchen was stifling. I was expecting our second child any day, and I had flour on my hands, apron, nose, and probably in my hair! It was a difficult and frustrating road to pie perfection for me until that July morning when "the one" came out of the oven.

I could hardly wait for the pie to cool. I touched the crust and realized it was perfectly flaky. I called Bill and his brother in from the barn and pleaded with them to try a piece of my freshly baked apple pie, even though we never ate dessert in the morning. There was silence as they each devoured the entire piece of pie and all the crust. I knew by the smile on Bill's face and the light in his eyes that I had done it! I had made him the perfect pie, finally.

When you read this story today, my accomplishment may not seem at all important. After all, pie is just a dessert to most folks and can be bought at any market. But a pie from scratch? Now that is a thing of beauty. It was only after I moved to the farm that I realized that part of the farming culture is being regularly called upon to whip up the perfect pie for a dinner, church fundraiser, or funeral meal. And so I willingly began to learn every domestic necessity to thrive in my new world on the potato farm. And it all started with a pie!

Apple Pie

YIELD: 1 DOUBLE-CRUST PIE

In the area around Georgian Bay, Ontario, local orchards grow McIntosh apples. They can also be found in grocery markets across Canada and the United States. I have found that they are the best apples for making pies.

Each autumn when my children were growing up, I took them to the packing house in Glencairn near our farm to buy apples by the bushel. The small apples were perfect for the kids to eat and take in their school lunches. I used them for juicing, too. The largest apples I used for making pies—the bigger the apple, the faster I could peel! McIntosh apples always bake to a smooth, silky texture and are naturally sweet and sour. Served with a slice of aged Canadian cheddar, this apple pie will create smiles all around the table!

. . . .

Pie crust recipe, page 104

7–8 large McIntosh apples, peeled, cored, and thinly sliced

Juice of ¼ lemon

½ cup granulated sugar

½ tsp ground nutmeg

1. Preheat the oven to 400°F.

2. Place the apple slices in a large bowl and sprinkle with the lemon juice. Lemon juice prevents the apples from turning brown.

3. In a smaller bowl, mix the sugar and nutmeg. Sprinkle over the apple slices. Toss to coat the slices evenly.

4. Fill an unbaked 9-inch pie crust. Heap the apples up, because they'll cook down during baking.

5. Gently drape the top crust over the apples. Using your fingers or a fork, pinch the top and bottom crust together at the edges to make a seal so no juices escape during baking. (If you use your fingers, flute the edges as you pinch.) With a knife, make a few small slashes in the top crust to allow steam to escape during baking.

6. Bake at 400°F for the first 10 minutes. Reduce the oven temperature to 350°F for 15 minutes, then reduce it again to 325°F for 45 minutes.

7. Cool the pie completely before serving. If you want to serve a warm slice of pie, it's important to first cool the pie to let the juice congeal before slicing; heat the slices in the microwave for a few minutes before serving.

→ **TIP** McIntosh is my absolute favourite, but for different flavours and textures, experiment with other kinds of apples to find the one you like. Granny Smith, Golden Delicious, Honeycrisp, Pink Lady, and Braeburn are all good choices.

Lemon Meringue Pie

YIELD: 1 SINGLE-CRUST PIE

The fresh lemon taste will have your family coming back for more! Make sure all ingredients are at room temperature.

1 ½ cups granulated sugar

6 Tbsp cornstarch

Dash sea salt

1 ½ cups hot filtered water

4 egg yolks, slightly beaten (reserve egg whites for meringue topping; see Tip)

2 Tbsp unsalted butter

⅓ cup fresh lemon juice

1 Tbsp lemon zest

½ pie crust recipe, blind-baked in a 9-inch pan and cooled (see recipe and Tip on pages 104–5)

¼ cup granulated sugar

½ tsp pure vanilla extract

½ tsp icing (confectioner's) sugar

1. Preheat the oven to 450°F.

2. Mix the 1½ cups granulated sugar, cornstarch, and salt in a saucepan. Slowly whisk in the hot water, making sure there are no lumps.

3. Bring to a boil, stirring constantly. When the mixture starts bubbling, continue to stir and cook 2 minutes more.

4. Transfer ¼ cup of the sugar mixture to a small bowl and whisk in the egg yolks. Add the egg mixture back into the saucepan and cook on medium-high until bubbly and thick.

5. Remove from the heat. Add the butter and lemon juice and stir until the butter melts. Add the lemon zest. Immediately transfer to the baked and cooled pie shell.

6. In a medium bowl, beat the egg whites until frothy. Add the ¼ cup sugar, vanilla, and icing sugar and beat on high until stiff peaks appear.

7. Pile the meringue overtop the warm lemon filling, spreading it to the pie crust edge. Use a rubber spatula to form peaks.

8. Bake for 5 to 10 minutes or until the meringue is lightly golden.

9. Cool to room temperature for at least 3 to 4 hours before serving. Refrigerating this pie is not recommended because it will lose its fresh taste and create unattractive moisture beads on the meringue topping.

→ **TIP** To separate the yolk from the egg white, set out two bowls. Break the egg into two equal halves over the bowl for the egg whites, being careful to keep the egg yolk in one of the halves. Some of the egg white will fall into the bowl. Cup the half shells, one in each hand. Empty out the shell without the egg yolk. Holding both halves slightly upright, gently slide the yolk back and forth into the half shells, allowing all the egg white to drain into the bowl. Empty the egg yolk into the second bowl.

Pumpkin Pie

YIELD: 1 SINGLE-CRUST PIE

This pumpkin pie recipe is truly an old-fashioned homemade favourite. The secret ingredient here is heavy cream. Using heavy cream instead of low-fat or evaporated milk creates a wonderfully smooth, silky texture with a rich taste. Eggs produce a custard-type pie, this one flavoured with nutmeg and a little cinnamon. I eat a slice for breakfast every so often just because there are three eggs in it!

....

PIE

3 large eggs

1 cup heavy cream

1 ¼ cups pumpkin purée (see Tip) or one 14 ½ oz can pure pumpkin purée

¾ cup packed brown sugar

½ tsp ground cinnamon

½ tsp ground nutmeg

Pinch sea salt

½ pie crust recipe, unbaked (see page 104)

TOPPING

1 cup heavy cream, chilled

½ tsp icing (confectioner's) sugar

¼ cup granulated sugar

½ tsp pure vanilla extract

1. Preheat the oven to 425°F.

2. Whisk the eggs in a large bowl until frothy. Add the cream and whisk constantly until thick and silky.

3. Stir in the pumpkin, brown sugar, cinnamon, nutmeg, and salt. Whisk until thoroughly blended.

4. Pour the filling into the uncooked pastry crust.

5. Bake at 425°F for the first 15 minutes, then reduce the oven temperature to 350°F and bake until the centre is firm, about 30 to 40 minutes or until a wooden pick comes out clean.

6. Cool completely on a wire rack and serve within 24 hours. Refrigerating pumpkin pie makes it soggy.

7. For the topping, both the bowl and the beaters should be cold before you start. Beat the chilled cream with an electric mixer on high speed.

8. Add the icing sugar and continue to beat.

9. Gradually add the granulated sugar and vanilla, whipping until peaks form.

10. Spread the whipped cream on top of the pie or place it in a separate bowl for individual serving.

→ **TIP** To make pumpkin purée from scratch, split a medium pumpkin crosswise and remove and discard seeds and fibres. Place the pumpkin, cut side down, on a lightly greased baking sheet. Bake at 325°F until tender, about 1 hour. Scrape the pulp away from the skin, then discard the skin. Place the pulp in a blender or food processor. Process in small batches until smooth. Push the purée through a coarse sieve. Measure 1 ¼ cups purée for each pumpkin pie recipe. Store the remaining purée, well covered, for up to 6 months in the freezer.

Lemon Curd Tarts

YIELD: 6-8 TARTS

Fresh lemons are the main ingredient in this recipe. The method is simple and results in a smooth and wonderful custard that you'll not only enjoy in tarts, but also want to use on just about everything (or devour on its own).

....

3 large eggs

¾ cup granulated sugar

⅓ cup fresh lemon juice (2-3 lemons)

¼ cup unsalted butter, softened

1 Tbsp lemon zest

6-8 baked tart shells

1. In a stainless-steel bowl or pan over a saucepan of simmering water, whisk the eggs, then add the sugar and lemon juice and continue to whisk until well blended.

2. Continue cooking, increasing the heat to medium and whisking constantly to prevent curdling. Cook until the mixture resembles a thick sauce with a consistency similar to sour cream, about 10 to 15 minutes. Use a candy thermometer to determine when the curd has reached the correct cooking temperature of 160°F.

3. Remove from the heat and immediately pour through a fine strainer to remove any lumps.

4. Cut the butter into small cubes and whisk, one at a time, into the warm mixture until melted.

5. Add the lemon zest, then allow the lemon curd to cool completely.

6. Fill the baked tarts with lemon curd, or cover the curd with plastic wrap and refrigerate for up to a week.

→ TIP Lemons at room temperature provide more juice. Strain the freshly squeezed juice to remove any pulp.

Zest is the yellow outer rind of the lemon. A zester or fine grater can be used to zest lemons, but do so right before you need the zest, since it will lose moisture if prepared too far in advance. Zest the lemon before juicing.

If you want to make these tarts entirely from scratch, use the pie crust recipe (see page 104). Roll out the pie dough, and use the mouth of a jar or a drinking glass to cut circles of pastry a little bigger than the tart tins. Gently transfer the pastry to the tins. Prick the bottom of the tart shells with a fork. Bake at 400°F for 5 minutes, then reduce the oven temperature to 300°F and bake for 10 more minutes or until golden brown. Cool completely before filling with lemon curd.

Raspberry Tarts

YIELD: 10-12 TARTS

These tarts are one of the best-loved desserts in our family. Bill loved raspberry tarts so much he could make one disappear in a single bite! He told me once that as a child he would help his mother pick raspberries from the berry patch behind their farmhouse. He knew he'd smell the aroma of fresh-baked berry tarts that day if he brought his mother a basket filled with fresh-picked raspberries!

....

1 pie crust recipe (see page 104), unbaked

2 cups fresh raspberries

½ cup granulated sugar

2 Tbsp cornstarch

2 Tbsp fresh lemon juice

1. Preheat the oven to 425°F.

2. Roll the pie dough thicker than for a pie. Use the mouth of a jar or a water glass to cut circles of pastry a little bigger than the tart tins. Gently transfer the pastry to the tins.

3. In a mixing bowl, crush the raspberries with a potato masher or fork. Transfer to a large mixing bowl.

4. Mix the raspberries with sugar, cornstarch, and lemon juice. Set aside. You may have some filling left over.

5. Fill each tart shell three-quarters full with raspberry filling. (You may have some filling left over.)

6. Bake the tarts for 5 minutes.

7. Reduce the oven temperature to 400°F and bake for 10 more minutes. Reduce the heat to 350°F and bake for an additional 10 minutes or until the filling bubbles and the pastry looks golden around the edges.

8. Cool completely. Carefully remove the tarts from the tin. Serve or transfer to an airtight container for up to 2 days.

→ **TIP** Small tart tins aren't always easy to find. Use individual aluminum-foil tart liners instead and arrange them in a muffin tin or set them carefully on a baking sheet—that will work just fine.

RASPBERRY PIE

Double the ingredients for the filling. Fill an unbaked 9-inch pie crust. Gently drape the top crust over the raspberries. Using your fingers or a fork, pinch the top and bottom crust together at the edges to make a seal so no juices escape during baking. (If you use your fingers, flute the edges as you pinch.) With a knife, make a few small slashes in the top crust to allow steam to escape during baking.

Bake at 400°F for the first 15 to 20 minutes. Reduce the oven to 350°F for 15 to 20 minutes, then reduce again to 300°F for 30 to 40 minutes. Cool the pie completely before cutting the first slice so the juice inside has time to congeal.

Freezer Jam 116

Berries in Syrup 117

Rhubarb Sauce 118

Freezer Sweet Corn Kernels 119

Pickled Beets 120

Garlic Dill Pickles 121

Preserving
AND
PICKLING

Freezer Jam

The fresh taste of summer can be preserved by crushing and freezing your family's favourite berries. It's easy, with no need to cook the jam or deal with hot water baths.

Strawberries, raspberries, and blackberries are easily transformed into a wonderful treat long after the berry season is a warm memory. Buy berries in season when they are ripe, taste the best, and are the least expensive. I like to make small jars of jam and give them as gifts at Christmas.

You'll need some glass preserving jars and lids. Before using, wash and sterilize the jars and lids in the dishwasher. Cool the jars completely, then set aside and cover with a tea towel until ready for filling.

. . . .

2 cups ripe strawberries, raspberries, or blackberries, crushed

4 cups granulated sugar

One 3 oz pouch liquid fruit pectin

2 Tbsp fresh lemon juice

1. Sterilize eight 4 oz preserving jars and lids (see recipe introduction).

2. Rinse and remove berry stems and leaves (and cut away any white pulp in strawberries).

3. In a large bowl, crush the berries well with a potato masher. Do not use a food processor.

4. Slowly stir in the sugar, adding and stirring until all the sugar has dissolved. I leave it overnight on the counter covered with a tea towel and stir it occasionally, just to make sure the sugar is dissolving. Skim and discard any foam. Stir until all sugar crystals disappear (usually by the next day).

5. In a small bowl, add the pouch of pectin and lemon juice and mix well.

6. Add the pectin mixture to the crushed berries and stir constantly for about 4 to 5 minutes.

7. Ladle the jam into the prepared jars almost to the top. Allow for expansion during freezing.

8. Let stand at room temperature for 24 hours. Check to make sure the jam has set before sealing the lids tightly. Store in the freezer for up to one year.

9. Thaw in the refrigerator before using. Opened jam will keep in the refrigerator for 3 to 6 weeks.

→ **TIP** The amount of sugar is critical to the jam setting. Reducing the amount will produce runny jam. If the jam doesn't set, transfer the runny jam into a large saucepan and heat slowly on low heat. If you reduced the amount of sugar during preparation, add more now and stir until dissolved. Cool and stir in 4 more Tbsp fruit pectin. Cool and ladle back into clean jars. Leave for another 12 hours and check to see if it has set. That should do it!

Push raspberry and blackberry jam through a sieve to remove the seeds. This will produce a jelly (and will reduce your yield).

Berries in Syrup

YIELD: TWO 16 OZ JARS

On a cold winter day, a jar of red raspberries is a taste of the summer! Serve with scones or ice cream.

....

4 cups raspberries
1 ½ cups filtered water
1 cup granulated sugar

1. Sterilize two 16 oz preserving jars and lids (see recipe introduction on the facing page).

2. Fill the jars carefully with whole raspberries almost to the rim.

3. In a small pan on medium-high heat, bring the water and sugar to a gentle boil, stirring and cooking for 2 to 3 minutes.

4. Pour enough hot syrup over the berries in each jar to about 1 inch from the top. This will allow room for expansion during freezing.

5. As you fill each jar, gently move the berries around with the long handle of a wooden spoon to allow air bubbles to escape, being careful not to damage any berries.

6. Seal and invert the jars and leave them on the counter overnight.

7. Turn the jars right side up the next day and leave on the counter for 12 more hours, then transfer to the freezer.

Rhubarb Sauce

Where we lived in Canada, almost every farmhouse had a patch of rhubarb growing out in the backyard. In early spring, the first shoots are tender and perfect for making delicious rhubarb sauce. Spread it cold on warm, buttered toast or pour it warm over vanilla ice cream. Or just fill a bowl and eat it with a spoon!

4–6 stalks rhubarb, washed, partly peeled, ends cut away, and chopped

2 cups filtered water

½–1 cup granulated sugar or to taste

¼ cup strawberry Freezer Jam (see page 116)

1. In a medium pot, cover the rhubarb with the water and bring to a boil.

2. Slowly add the sugar, stirring until dissolved.

3. Reduce the heat and simmer for 30 minutes or until the rhubarb is completely cooked, stirring occasionally and adding more water if needed.

4. Continue cooking and reduce to sauce consistency.

5. Remove from the heat, cool, and stir in the strawberry jam.

6. Store in a covered container and refrigerate for up to a week, or freeze in freezer bags or sterilized glass jars (see recipe introduction on page 116) for up to 2 months.

Freezer Sweet Corn Kernels

YIELD: 6 CUPS

A bit about corn, then and now: maize was developed from a wild grass called teosinte, found in southern Mexico seven thousand years ago. The ancestral kernels of teosinte looked very different from today's corn.

Organically grown corn that is non-GMO is a wise choice. This freezer recipe preserves the taste of sweet corn on the cob to add to meals all winter long.

. . . .

6 ears sweet corn
1 cup filtered water
2 tsp brown or granulated sugar or honey

1. Preheat the oven to 350°F.

2. Husk and clean the corn.

3. Use a sharp knife to remove the kernels from the cob. Starting at the thickest part of the cob, run the blade down to the narrow end. Place the kernels in a bowl.

4. In a small bowl, mix the water and sugar or honey. Add to the kernels and stir.

5. Transfer all to a baking pan and spread out evenly. The baking pan should be large enough to hold one layer of the corn.

6. Bake in the preheated oven for 15 to 20 minutes, turning the kernels over occasionally to distribute the water evenly while baking.

7. Cool completely.

8. Fill sterilized glass jars (see recipe introduction on page 116) or freezer bags in portions that you'll use for future meals, and freeze for up to 4 months.

→ **TIP** Lay filled freezer bags on a baking sheet and freeze flat, then store.

Pickled Beets

YIELD: FOUR 16 OZ JARS

Grandma Kerr always preserved beets in season this way. For two days or more, her kitchen was filled with the aroma of pickling spices and vinegar while she "put up" enough jars of beets to last the long Canadian winter.

. . . .

6–8 medium fresh beets

2 cups granulated sugar

2 cups cider vinegar

1 tsp pickling salt (not table salt)

2 sticks cinnamon

1 Tbsp whole allspice

3 Tbsp pickling spice

8 whole cloves

1. Sterilize four 16 oz preserving jars with lids (see recipe introduction on page 116, but you don't have to cool down the jars).

2. Scrub the beets well. Remove soil and cut away the stalks and leaves, leaving the stem (about 1 inch) and root intact. Cover the beets with water in a large stockpot.

3. Bring the water to a boil and cook until fork-tender, about 45 to 55 minutes.

4. Transfer 2 cups of the beet water to a small pan. Set aside.

5. Remove the beet skins under cold running water when the beets are cool enough to handle. Use a paring knife to slice away the stems and roots. Slice the beets in quarters or sixths and set aside.

6. Bring the beet water, sugar, vinegar, pickling salt, cinnamon, allspice, and pickling spice to a boil. Simmer for 15 to 20 minutes or until beets are cooked when you test them with a fork.

7. Transfer the sliced beets to warm jars and add two cloves to each jar.

8. Pour enough hot liquid to cover the beets, then seal the jars. Cool overnight.

9. Refrigerate for a week before tasting. Store in the fridge.

→ **TIP** Wear plastic gloves while peeling and slicing the beets to prevent staining your skin.

Garlic Dill Pickles

YIELD: FOUR 16 OZ OR TWO 32 OZ JARS

Make these pickles over two days and store for at least six weeks before tasting.

....

2 lb small pickling (not regular) cucumbers

½ cup pickling salt (not table salt)

4 large sprigs fresh dillweed

1 ½ cups white vinegar, 5% acidity

10–12 cloves garlic, sliced in halves or quarters

16 peppercorns

1. Select firm, fresh cucumbers and wash thoroughly. Remove a small slice from each end. Puncture them all over with a fork.

2. Transfer the cucumbers to a glass or ceramic bowl (it's important not to use reactive steel or metal). Cover the cucumbers with pickling salt.

3. Cover with water. Use a plate if needed to push the cucumbers down into the water.

4. Set on the counter overnight or for up to 24 hours.

5. The next day, sterilize four 16 oz or two 32 oz glass preserving jars and lids (see recipe introduction on page 116 but do not let them cool down). Large cucumbers can be sliced to fit your jars.

6. Wash the dillweed and air-dry.

7. Rinse the cucumbers under tap water two or three times to remove the salt.

8. Bring 1 cup filtered water and the vinegar to a boil and continue to boil for 1 full minute.

9. Divide the dill, garlic, and peppercorns into four portions.

10. While the jars are still hot, stuff with the dillweed, garlic, and peppercorns. Fill tightly with whole or sliced cucumbers or cucumber spears.

11. Cover with the hot vinegar mixture. Use the handle of a wooden spoon to poke around between the cucumbers and remove any air bubbles.

12. Wipe the jar rims clean. Seal the lids.

13. Cool on the kitchen counter for 48 hours.

14. Transfer to the refrigerator. Store for 6 weeks before tasting and up to a year unopened.

METRIC CONVERSION CHARTS

WEIGHT

IMPERIAL OR U.S.	METRIC
1 oz	30 g
2 oz	60 g
3 oz	85 g
4 oz	115 g
5 oz	140 g
6 oz	170 g
7 oz	200 g
8 oz (½ lb)	225 g
9 oz	255 g
10 oz	285 g
11 oz	310 g
12 oz	340 g
13 oz	370 g
14 oz	400 g
15 oz	425 g
16 oz (1 lb)	455 g
2 lb	910 g

CANS AND CANNING JARS

IMPERIAL OR U.S.	METRIC
4 oz	114 mL/125 mL
8 oz	250 mL
14 oz	398 mL
16 oz	500 mL
28 oz	796 mL
32 oz	1 L

VOLUME

IMPERIAL OR U.S.	METRIC
¼ tsp	1 mL
½ tsp	2.5 mL
¾ tsp	4 mL
1 tsp	5 mL
1 Tbsp	15 mL
1½ Tbsp	23 mL
2 Tbsp	30 mL
¼ cup	60 mL
⅓ cup	80 mL
½ cup	120 mL
⅔ cup	160 mL
¾ cup	180 mL
1 cup	240 mL
1¼ cups	300 mL
1⅓ cups	320 mL
1½ cups	355 mL
1⅔ cups	400 mL
1¾ cups	420 mL
2 cups	480 mL
2¼ cups	535 mL
2½ cups	600 mL
2¾ cups	660 mL
3 cups	720 mL
4 cups	960 mL

LENGTH

IMPERIAL OR U.S.	METRIC
¼ inch	6 mm
½ inch	12 mm
¾ inch	2 cm
1 inch	2.5 cm
1¼ inches	3 cm
1½ inches	3.5 cm
1¾ inches	4.5 cm
2 inches	5 cm
3 inches	7.5 cm
4 inches	10 cm
5 inches	12.5 cm
6 inches	15 cm
7 inches	18 cm
8 inches	20 cm
9 inches	23 cm
10 inches	25 cm
12 inches	30 cm

TEMPERATURE

IMPERIAL OR U.S.	METRIC
120°F	49°c
140°F	60°c
160°F	71°c
180°F	82°c
250°F	120°c
275°F	135°c
300°F	150°c
325°F	160°c
350°F	180°c
375°F	190°c
400°F	200°c
425°F	220°c
450°F	230°c
500°F	260°c

INDEX

Page references in italics indicate a photograph.

Anaheim peppers
    Salsa, 6
appetizers
    Artichoke Spinach Dip, *4, 5*
    Devilled Eggs, 8, 9
    Guacamole, 7
    Salsa, 6
    Tomato Basil Bruschetta, *2, 3*
apple(s)
    Crisp, 79
    Pie, 106, *107*
    -Stuffed Pork Loin Roast, 68
Artichoke Spinach Dip, *4, 5*
asparagus
    Cauliflower Salad, 18, *19*
avocados
    Guacamole, 7

bacon
    Easy Spinach Salad, 12
    Twice-Baked Potatoes, *34, 35*
Baked Wild Salmon, 69
baking. *See* desserts and baking
Banana Muffins, *100*, 101
Basic Scone Mix, 94
basil
    Garlic Croutons, 22
    Tomato Bruschetta, *2, 3*
beef
    buying a steer, 61
    Corned, and Cabbage,
        58–59, *59*
    Kowalski Cabbage Rolls,
        48, 49
    and Macaroni Casserole,
        52, 53
    Meatloaf, 56
    Prime Rib au Jus, 60
    Shepherd's Pie, 50, *51*
    Spaghetti Sauce, 57
    Stew, Irish Canadian, *46, 47*
Beets, Pickled, 120
bell peppers
    Quinoa Pilaf, 36, *37*
    Spaghetti Sauce, 57
Berries in Syrup, 117
Best Pie Crust, 104–5
Bill's Pan-Fried
    Potatoes, 26, *27*
Biscuits, Tea, 93

blackberry(ies)
    Freezer Jam, 116
blue cheese
    Iceberg Lettuce Salad, 13
bocconcini
    Easy Spinach Salad, 12
Boiled New Potatoes with
    Butter, 24–25
Bran Muffins, 102, *103*
Brownies, Grandma Kerr's, 87
Bruschetta, Tomato Basil, *2, 3*
buttermilk
    Iceberg Lettuce Salad, 13
    One-Bowl Birthday Cake, 92

cabbage
    chopping, 16 (tip)
    Corned Beef and, 58–59, *59*
    Rolls, Kowalski, *48, 49*
    Salad, 16, *19*
    Shrimp Tacos, 73
    Vegetable Soup, 41
cake(s)
    Carrot, *88, 89*
    Flourless Chocolate, 90, *91*
    One-Bowl Birthday, 92
carrot(s)
    Cabbage Salad, 16, *19*
    Cake, *88, 89*
    Chicken Stock, 40
    Corned Beef and Cabbage,
        58–59, *59*
    French Canadian Pea Soup,
        44, 45
    Irish Canadian Beef Stew,
        46, 47
    Quinoa Pilaf, 36, *37*
    Vegetable Soup, 41
cashews
    Vickie's Baked Granola, *96, 97*
casserole(s)
    Kowalski Cabbage Rolls,
        48, 49
    Macaroni and Beef, *52, 53*
    Shepherd's Pie, 50, *51*
Cauliflower Salad, 18, *19*
celery
    Chicken Stock, 40
    Egg Salad, 17
    French Canadian Pea
        Soup, *44, 45*
    Irish Canadian Beef
        Stew, *46, 47*

    Potato Salad, 23
    Quinoa Pilaf, 36, *37*
    Spaghetti Sauce, 57
    Vickie's Tuna Salad, *20, 21*
cheddar cheese
    Twice-Baked Potatoes, *34, 35*
cheese. *See specific types*
chicken
    Kiev, *64, 65*
    Roast, and Gravy, 66, 67
    Stock, 40
chips
    chip-stock potatoes,
        29, 31 (tip)
    Chocolate-Covered Potato
        Chips, 76, 77
    Potato Chip Chocolate
        Squares, 78
    Vickie's Potato Chips, *30, 31*
chocolate. *See also* cocoa
    Cake, Flourless, 90, *91*
    Chip and Nut Cookies, *82, 83*
    Covered Potato Chips, 76, 77
    Nanaimo Bars, *80, 81*
    Potato Chip Squares, 78
cilantro
    Salsa, 6
    Shrimp Tacos, 73
cocoa. *See also* chocolate
    Grandma Kerr's Brownies, 87
    Nanaimo Bars, *80, 81*
    One-Bowl Birthday Cake, 92
    Potato Chip Chocolate
        Squares, 78
coconut
    Granddad's Cookies, 84
    Nanaimo Bars, *80, 81*
    Potato Chip Chocolate
        Squares, 78
    Vickie's Baked Granola, *96, 97*
coleslaw, 16, *19*
cookies
    Chocolate Chip and Nut, *82, 83*
    Granddad's, 84
    Oatmeal Raisin, 86
    Shortbread, 85
corn
    Kernels, Freezer Sweet, 119
    Shepherd's Pie, 50, *51*
Corned Beef and Cabbage,
    58–59, *59*
cranberry(ies)
    Kale and Spinach Salad, *14, 15*

    Orange Scones, 94, 95
    Vickie's Baked Granola, *96, 97*
cream
    Cranberry Orange Scones,
        94, 95
    Nanaimo Bars, *80, 81*
    Pumpkin Pie, 109
    Tea Biscuits, 93
cream cheese
    Artichoke Spinach Dip, *4, 5*
    Carrot Cake, *88, 89*
Creamy Garlic Whipped
    Potatoes, 28
Croutons, Garlic Basil, 22
cucumbers
    Garlic Dill Pickles, 121

desserts and baking
    Apple Crisp, 79
    Apple Pie, 106, *107*
    Banana Muffins, *100*, 101
    Best Pie Crust, 104–5
    Bran Muffins, 102, *103*
    Carrot Cake, *88, 89*
    Chocolate Chip and Nut
        Cookies, *82, 83*
    Chocolate-Covered Potato
        Chips, 76, 77
    Cranberry Orange
        Scones, 94, 95
    Flourless Chocolate
        Cake, 90, *91*
    Granddad's Cookies, 84
    Grandma Kerr's Brownies, 87
    Lemon Curd Tarts, *110*, 111
    Lemon Meringue Pie, 108
    Nanaimo Bars, *80, 81*
    Oatmeal Raisin Cookies, 86
    One-Bowl Birthday Cake, 92
    Potato Chip Chocolate
        Squares, 78
    Pumpkin Pie, 109
    Raspberry Tarts, 112, *113*
    Shortbread Cookies, 85
    Tea Biscuits, 93
    Vickie's Baked Granola, *96, 97*
    Zucchini Loaf, 98, *99*
Devilled Eggs, 8, 9
Dill Pickles, Garlic, 121
dip(s)
    Artichoke Spinach, *4, 5*
    Guacamole, 7
    Salsa, 6

Easy Spinach Salad, 12
egg(s)
    Devilled, 8, 9
    Easy Spinach Salad, 12
    hard-boiling and peeling, 8
    Potato Salad, 23
    Salad, 17
    separating yolk from
        white, 108 (tip)

Fish and Chips, 70, 71–72
flaxseeds
    Bran Muffins, 102, 103
    Vickie's Baked Granola, 96, 97
Flourless Chocolate Cake, 90, 91
Freezer Jam, 116
freezing stock, 40 (tip)
French Canadian Pea Soup, 44, 45
French-Fried Potatoes, 70, 72
French Onion Soup, 42, 43

garlic
    Basil Croutons, 22
    Dill Pickles, 121
    Spareribs, Montreal
        Dry, 62, 63
    Whipped Potatoes,
        Creamy, 28
ginger
    Montreal Dry Garlic
        Spareribs, 62, 63
graham wafer crumbs
    Nanaimo Bars, 80, 81
Granddad's Cookies, 84
Grandma Kerr's Brownies, 87
Granola, Vickie's Baked, 96, 97
Gravy, Roast Chicken and, 66, 67
Gruyère cheese
    French Onion Soup, 42, 43
Guacamole, 7

ham
    French Canadian Pea Soup,
        44, 45
hard-boiling and peeling eggs, 8

Iceberg Lettuce Salad, 13
imperial to metric conversions,
    122–23
Irish Canadian Beef Stew, 46, 47

jalapeño peppers
    Salsa, 6

Jam, Freezer, 116

Kale and Spinach Salad, 14, 15
Kowalski Cabbage Rolls, 48, 49

lemon(s)
    Baked Wild Salmon, 69
    Curd Tarts, 110, 111
    juicing and zesting, 111 (tip)
    Meringue Pie, 108
lettuce
    Iceberg, Salad, 13
    Wild Salmon Salad, 22

macaroni
    and Beef Casserole, 52, 53
    Vickie's Tuna Salad, 20, 21
main dishes. See meat
    and seafood
meat and seafood.
    See also specific types
    Apple-Stuffed Pork Loin
        Roast, 68
    Baked Wild Salmon, 69
    Chicken Kiev, 64, 65
    Corned Beef and Cabbage,
        58–59, 59
    Fish and Chips, 70, 71–72
    Meatloaf, 56
    Montreal Dry Garlic
        Spareribs, 62, 63
    Prime Rib au Jus, 60
    Roast Chicken and
        Gravy, 66, 67
    Shrimp Tacos, 73
    Spaghetti Sauce, 57
metric to imperial
    conversions, 122–23
milk
    Banana Muffins, 101
    Bran Muffins, 102, 103
    Creamy Garlic Whipped
        Potatoes, 28
    curdling, 101 (tip)
    Meatloaf, 56
    One-Bowl Birthday
        Cake, 92
    Shepherd's Pie, 50, 51
    Tea Biscuits, 93
mincemeat
    Bran Muffins, 102, 103
Monterey Jack cheese
    Chicken Kiev, 64, 65

mozzarella cheese
    Artichoke Spinach Dip, 4, 5
muffins
    Banana, 100, 101
    Bran, 102, 103

Nanaimo Bars, 80, 81

Oatmeal Raisin Cookies, 86
oats
    Apple Crisp, 79
    Granddad's Cookies, 84
    Oatmeal Raisin Cookies, 86
    Vickie's Baked Granola, 96, 97
One-Bowl Birthday Cake, 92
Onion Soup, French, 42, 43
Orange Cranberry Scones, 94, 95
Oven-Roasted Herb
    Potatoes, 32, 33

Parmesan cheese
    Artichoke Spinach Dip, 4, 5
    Chicken Kiev, 64, 65
    Kale and Spinach Salad, 14, 15
    Meatloaf, 56
parsley
    Baked Wild Salmon, 69
    Cauliflower Salad, 18, 19
    Meatloaf, 56
pasta. See also Spaghetti Sauce
    Macaroni and Beef Casserole,
        52, 53
    Vickie's Tuna Salad, 20, 21
pea(s)
    Soup, French Canadian, 44, 45
    Vickie's Tuna Salad, 20, 21
pecans
    Apple Crisp, 79
    Chocolate Chip and Nut
        Cookies, 82, 83
    Iceberg Lettuce Salad, 13
    Vickie's Baked Granola, 96, 97
peppers. See Anaheim peppers;
    bell peppers; jalapeño
    peppers
pickles
    Garlic Dill, 121
    Pickled Beets, 120
pie(s)
    Apple, 106, 107
    Crust, Best, 104–5
    Lemon Meringue, 108
    Pumpkin, 109

Raspberry, 112
pork. See also bacon; ham
    Apple-Stuffed Loin Roast, 68
    Kowalski Cabbage Rolls,
        48, 49
    Montreal Dry Garlic
        Spareribs, 62, 63
potassium nitrate
    Corned Beef and Cabbage,
        58–59, 59
potato(es)
    Boiled New, with Butter, 24–25
    boiling, 28 (tip)
    Chip Chocolate Squares, 78
    Chips, Chocolate-Covered,
        76, 77
    Chips, Vickie's, 30, 31
    chip-stock, 29, 31 (tip)
    Corned Beef and Cabbage,
        58–59, 59
    French-Fried, 70, 72
    growing and selling,
        24–25, 29
    Irish Canadian Beef Stew,
        46, 47
    Oven-Roasted Herb, 32, 33
    Pan-Fried, Bill's, 26, 27
    roasting, 33 (tip)
    Salad, 23
    Shepherd's Pie, 50, 51
    Twice-Baked, 34, 35
    Whipped, Creamy Garlic, 28
preserves
    Berries in Syrup, 117
    Freezer Jam, 116
    Freezer Sweet Corn
        Kernels, 119
    Rhubarb Sauce, 118
Prime Rib au Jus, 60
Pumpkin Pie, 109

Quinoa Pilaf, 36, 37

raisin(s)
    Carrot Cake, 88, 89
    Iceberg Lettuce Salad, 13
    Oatmeal Cookies, 86
    Vickie's Baked Granola, 96, 97
    Zucchini Loaf, 98, 99
raspberry(ies)
    Berries in Syrup, 117
    Freezer Jam, 116
    Pie, 112

Tarts, 112, *113*
Rhubarb Sauce, 118
rice
    Kowalski Cabbage
        Rolls, *48, 49*
Romano cheese
    Artichoke Spinach Dip, *4,* 5

salad dressing (Miracle Whip)
    Artichoke Spinach Dip, *4,* 5
    Cabbage Salad, 16, *19*
    Devilled Eggs, 8, *9*
    Egg Salad, 17
    Iceberg Lettuce Salad, 13
    Potato Salad, 23
    Vickie's Tuna Salad, *20, 21*
salad(s)
    Cabbage, 16, *19*
    Cauliflower, 18, *19*
    Easy Spinach, 12
    Egg, 17
    Iceberg Lettuce, 13
    Kale and Spinach, *14, 15*
    Potato, 23
    Vickie's Tuna, *20, 21*
    Wild Salmon, 22
salmon
    Baked Wild, 69
    Salad, Wild, 22
Salsa, 6
scone(s)
    Basic Mix, 94
    Cranberry Orange, 94, *95*
seafood. *See* meat and
    seafood
Shepherd's Pie, 50, *51*
Shortbread Cookies, 85
Shrimp Tacos, 73
side dishes
    Bill's Pan-Fried
        Potatoes, 26, *27*
    Boiled New Potatoes with
        Butter, 24–25
    Creamy Garlic Whipped
        Potatoes, 28
    Oven-Roasted Herb
        Potatoes, *32, 33*
    Quinoa Pilaf, 36, *37*
    Twice-Baked Potatoes, *34,* 35
    Vickie's Potato Chips, *30, 31*
soup(s)
    Chicken Stock, 40
    French Canadian Pea, *44, 45*

French Onion, 42, *43*
Vegetable, 41
sour cream
    Kowalski Cabbage Rolls,
        48, 49
    Twice-Baked Potatoes,
        34, 35
    Spaghetti Sauce, 57
spinach
    Artichoke Dip, *4,* 5
    and Kale Salad, *14, 15*
    Salad, Easy, 12
    Vegetable Soup, 41
    Wild Salmon Salad, 22
Stew, Irish Canadian Beef, 46, *47*
Stock, Chicken, 40
strawberry(ies)
    Freezer Jam, 116
sugar
    amount for jam, 116 (tip)
    brown, keeping soft, 92 (tip)
sunflower seeds
    Vickie's Baked Granola, 96, *97*

Tacos, Shrimp, 73
tarts
    Lemon Curd, *110,* 111
    Raspberry, 112, *113*
Tea Biscuits, 93
tomato(es)
    Basil Bruschetta, *2, 3*
    Iceberg Lettuce Salad, 13
    Kale and Spinach Salad, *14, 15*
    Macaroni and Beef
        Casserole, 52, *53*
    Meatloaf, 56
    Salsa, 6
    Spaghetti Sauce, 57
    Vegetable Soup, 41
    Wild Salmon Salad, 22
Tuna Salad, Vickie's, *20, 21*
Twice-Baked Potatoes, *34,* 35

Vegetable Soup, 41
Vickie's Baked Granola, 96, *97*
Vickie's Potato Chips, *30, 31*
Vickie's Tuna Salad, *20, 21*

walnuts
    Carrot Cake, *88,* 89
    Cranberry Orange
        Scones, 94, *95*
    Kale and Spinach Salad, *14, 15*

Vickie's Baked Granola, 96, *97*
Zucchini Loaf, 98, *99*
wheat germ
    Bran Muffins, 102, *103*
    Oatmeal Raisin Cookies, 86
Wild Salmon Salad, 22

zucchini
    Loaf, 98, *99*
    Vegetable Soup, 41

VICKIE KERR is an entrepreneur and creator of the Miss Vickie's brand of potato chips. She launched the brand in 1987 after creating an original recipe that used potatoes her husband, Bill, grew on their farm. Vickie is also a dedicated home cook and advocate for the idea of creating a family legacy through food. She believes everyone can cook healthy, delicious meals at home and that they are meant to be shared around the table with family and friends. This is her first book. She divides her time between Arizona and Ontario.

DEAR MISS VICKIE

THANK YOU VERY MUCH FOR THE
BEST CHIPS EVER. THEY ARE GREAT!

I AM AN OLD CHIP LOVER BUT NOW I AM
SPOILED THAT I DON'T LIKE THE TASTE
OF ANY OTHER KIND ANY LONGER.

THE ONLY PRESENT PROBLEM IS THAT
THEY ARE SOMETIMES HARD TO FIND SO WHEN
I LOCATE A STORE THAT SELLS THEM I MUST
… UP.
— DO NOT

Dear Miss Vickie's   July 14/89
Your chips are
so delicious! My Best frie...
I got a big bag and
same night we ate the...
I think your chips are
best in the ~~business~~ b...
they are so crunchy a...
and I feel like eating
whenever I ~~what~~ ...
...ips I have Miss V...
will never st...
buying them!
...want case
to write back!

...s Vickie's
...2 #2
...n Lowell, Ontario

...r Miss Vickie,
   I have tried differen...
...otato chips before and yours
...No. 1. Aside from rich...
...min C and cholesterol free ta...
...crunchiness is superb compare...
...chips that I have tasted...
...now on I'll stick to your c...

March 26/90

Dear Miss Vickie
   or Whom it May Concern.
   It was given some of your chips to
sample by a friend, I found them
absolutely delicious, fresh, tasty, just
wonderful.
   I run a bar-restaurant in Montreal and
purchased several bags from my local
Provigo Store - (so happy to find them there
I served some to my customers for
happy hour, the customers, as I were
unanimous in saying how wonderful
your chips were.
   I have since bought them several times
and given them to friends. Everyone
thinks they are just wonderful.
   You certainly have lots of ...
here in Montreal, myself ...
now a regular buy...
   Keep u...
MARCH 28/90

Miss and Mr. Vickie's
R. R. # 2
New Lowell, Ontario
LOM 1NO

Dear Miss Vickie:
   I wanted to write and tell you how delicious your Miss
chips are. I am a true chip lover and recently discovered you...
at a store called Scatallons Deli in Grimsby, Ontario. I love...
and the lack of additives and preservatives. Thank you for your efforts.
...sure.   Sincerely,

Dear Miss Vickie,
to write and let you
much I love your
e always eaten
MPTY". But yours are
better. There are
stores that sell yo
chips. I always
special trip and
rent but i just so
em, the flavour is
le. THANK YOU.
p up the good w

Dear Miss Vickie
I AM SITTING HERE EATING
YOUR DELICIOUS CHIPS. MY PREFERENCE
IS THE ONES WITH THE SEA SALT.
I HOPE YOU NEVER CHANGE YOUR
METHOD. BECAUSE THEY ARE PERFECT.
I HOPE THE AIM FOR HIGHER PROFITS
WILL NOT ENTICE YOU TO SELL YOUR
FORMULA TO THE LARGE CHIP COMPANIES.
BECAUSE THEY DO NOT KNOW HOW TO
MAKE GOOD CHIPS NOW. THEY WOULD
TAKE YOUR FORMULA AND H—
THAT YOU PUT INTO THIS
EXCELLENT CHIPS. AND DE—
EFFORTS IN THE FIRST BA—
BIG DOES NOT ALWAYS MEAN
BEING SMALL AND MAKING AN—
PRODUCT DOES. BRING PROFIT.
KEEP UP THE GOO—
BEST REG—
Helen Cu—

DEAR MISS Vic
WITHOUT A C
OUTSTANDING
about your EHi
FROM THE VERY
this summer. S
but miss Vickie
I bring four o
Well, guess wha
to miss Vickies

I recently read
how you started
you is T —

Dear Miss Vickie:
We have just finished
(almost) an entire 180 gr
Bag of your delicious
hand-dipped potato chip
in less than 10 minutes
Could this be an
addiction?
Why can't I stop eating
them? They are too goo
Please send more.

Dear Miss Vickie's
Your potato chips are a clean
refreshing change to the oiled-d—
greased-down synthetic taste of
snacks today. "

Dear Miss Vickie's!
Their Great!!
I'm a chip lover; everyday
I eat a bag of potato
chips - a friend of mine
at work had bought
"Miss Vickie's Hand Cooked

Dear Miss Vickie,
I want to congratulate
n your potato chips.
the best I have e—
I start eating

9/25/89
DEAR MISS VICKIE
THANK YOU VERY MUCH FOR THE
BEST CHIPS EVER. THEY ARE GREAT!